YOUR FAITH IS YOUR FORTUNE

Neville Goddard

CLASSY
PUBLISHING

YOUR FAITH IS YOUR FORTUNE
by Neville Goddard

Published by Classy Publishing, 2023

www.classypublishing.com
info@classypublishing.com

ISBN: 978-93-5522-320-3

Typeset in Minion Pro
Cover Design by Classy Publishing

Man's faith in God is measured by his confidence in himself.

—Neville Goddard

CONTENTS

CHAPTER 1

Before Abraham Was

Verily, verily, I say unto you, before Abraham was, I AM.

—John 8:58

In the beginning was the Word, and the Word was with God, and the Word was God.

—John 1:1

In the beginning was the unconditioned awareness of being, and the unconditioned awareness of being became conditioned by imagining itself to be something, and the unconditioned awareness of being became that which it had imagined itself to be; so did creation begin.

By this law – first conceiving, then becoming that conceived – all things evolve out of No-thing; and without this sequence there is not anything made that is made.

Before Abraham or the world was – I AM. When all of time shall cease to be – I AM. I AM the formless awareness of being conceiving myself to be man. By my everlasting law of being I am compelled to be and to express all that I believe myself to be.

I AM the eternal No-thing-ness containing within my formless self the capacity to be all things.

I AM that in which all my conceptions of myself live and move and have their being, and apart from which they are not.

I dwell within every conception of myself; from this within-ness, I ever seek to transcend all conceptions of myself. By the very law of my being, I transcend my conceptions of myself, only as I believe myself to be that which does transcend.

I AM the law of being and beside ME there is no law. I AM that I AM.

CHAPTER 2

You Shall Decree

Thou shalt also decree a thing and it shall be established unto thee and the light shall shine upon thy ways.

> *You will also decree a thing, and it will be established for you; And light will shine on your ways. Thou shalt decree a thing, and it I shall come to thee, and light shall shine in thy ways.*
>
> —Job 22:28

> *So shall My word be that goeth forth out of My mouth; it shall not return unto Me void, but it shall accomplish that which I please, and it shall prosper in the thing whereto I sent it.*
>
> —Isaiah 55:11

Man can decree a thing and it will come to pass.

Man has always decreed that which has appeared in his world. He is today decreeing that which is appearing in his world and he shall continue to do so as long as man is conscious of being man.

Nothing has ever appeared in man's world, but what man decreed that it should. This you may deny; but try as you will, you cannot disprove it for this decreeing is based upon a changeless principle.

Man does not command things to appear by his words, which are, more often than not, a confession of his doubts and fears.

Decreeing is ever done in consciousness.

Every man automatically expresses that which he is conscious of being. Without effort or the use of words, at every moment of time, man is commanding himself to be and to possess that which he is conscious of being and possessing.

This changeless principle of expression is dramatized in all the Bibles of the world. The writers of our sacred books were illumined mystics, past masters in the art of psychology. In telling the story of the soul, they personified this impersonal principle in the form of a historical document both to preserve it and to hide it from the eyes of the uninitiated.

Today, those to whom this great treasure has been entrusted, namely, the priesthoods of the world, have forgotten that the Bibles are psychological dramas representing the consciousness of man; in their blind forgetfulness, they now teach their followers to worship its characters as men and women who actually lived in time and space.

When man sees the Bible as a great psychological drama, with all of its characters and actors as the personified qualities and attributes of his own consciousness, then – and then only – will the Bible reveal to him the light of its symbology.

This Impersonal principle of life which made all things is personified as God.

This Lord God, creator of heaven and earth, is discovered to be man's awareness of being.

If man were less bound by orthodoxy and more intuitively observant, he could not fail to notice in the reading of the Bibles that the awareness of being is revealed hundreds of times throughout this literature.

To name a few:

I AM hath sent me unto you.

—Exodus 3:14

Be still and know that I AM God.

—Psalm 46:10

I AM the Lord and there is no other God.
I am the LORD, and there is none else, there is no God beside Me.

—Isaiah 45:5

I am the LORD your God, and there is no other.

—Joel 2:27

I AM the shepherd.
I am the good shepherd: the good shepherd giveth His life for the sheep.

—John 10:11

I am the good shepherd, and know My sheep, and am known of Mine.

—John 10:14

I AM the door.
I am the door: by Me if any man enter in, he shall be saved, and shall go in and out, and find pasture.

—John 10:9

Verily, verily, I say unto you, I am the door of the sheep.

—John 10:7

I AM the resurrection and the life.

—John 11:25

I AM the way.
I am the way, and the truth, and the life; no one cometh to the Father but through Me.

—John 14:6

I AM the beginning and the end.
I am Alpha and Omega, the beginning and the end, the first and the last.

—Revelation 22:13

I am Alpha and Omega, the beginning and the ending, saith the Lord, Which is, and Which was, and Which is to come, the Almighty.

—Revelation 1:8

I AM; man's unconditioned awareness of being is revealed as Lord and Creator of every conditioned state of being.

If man would give up his belief in a God apart from himself, recognize his awareness of being to be God (this awareness fashions itself in the likeness and image of its conception of itself), he would transform his world from a barren waste to a fertile field of his own liking.

The day man does this he will know that he and his Father are one, but his Father is greater than he. He will know that his consciousness of being is one with that which he is conscious of being, but that his unconditioned consciousness of being is greater than his conditioned state or his conception of himself.

When man discovers his consciousness to be the impersonal power of expression, which power eternally personifies itself in his conceptions of himself, he will assume and appropriate that state of consciousness which he desires to express; in so doing he will become that state in expression.

"Ye shall decree a thing and it shall come to pass" can now be told in this manner: You shall become conscious of being or possessing a thing and you shall express or possess that which you are conscious of being.

The law of consciousness is the only law of expression.

"I AM the way." "I AM the resurrection."

Consciousness is the way as well as the power which resurrects and expresses all that man will ever be conscious of being.

Turn from the blindness of the uninitiated man who attempts to express and possess those qualities and things which he is not conscious of being and possessing; and be as the illumined mystic who decrees on the basis of this changeless law. Consciously claim yourself to be that which you seek; appropriate the consciousness of that which you see; and you too will know the status of the true mystic, as follows:

I became conscious of being it. I am still conscious of being it. And I shall continue to be conscious of being it until that which I am conscious of being is perfectly expressed.

Yes, I shall decree a thing and it shall come to pass.

CHAPTER 3

The Principle of Truth

Ye shall know the truth, and the truth shall make you free.

—John 8:32

The truth that sets man free is the knowledge that his consciousness is the resurrection and the life, that his consciousness both resurrects and makes alive all that he is conscious of being.

Apart from consciousness, there is neither resurrection nor life.

When man gives up his belief in a God apart from himself and begins to recognize his awareness of being to be God, as did Jesus and the prophets, he will transform his world with the realization,

I and My Father are one.

—John 10:30

but

My Father is greater than I.

—John 14:28

He will know that his consciousness is God and that which he is conscious of being is the Son bearing witness of God, the Father.

The conceiver and the conception are one, but the conceiver is greater than his conception. Before Abraham was, I AM. Yes, I was aware of being before I became aware of being man, and in that day when I shall cease to be conscious of being man I shall still be conscious of being.

The consciousness of being is not dependent upon being anything.

It preceded all conceptions of itself and shall be when all conceptions of itself shall cease to be. "I AM the beginning and the end". That is, all things or conceptions of myself begin and end in me, but I, the formless awareness, remain forever.

Jesus discovered this glorious truth and declared Himself to be one with God, not the God that man had fashioned, for He never recognized such a God.

Jesus found God to be His awareness of being and so told man that the Kingdom of God and Heaven were within [Luke 17:21,23].

When it is recorded that Jesus left the world and went to His Father — "He was received up into heaven" [Mark 16:19, Luke 24:51] — it is simply stating that He turned His attention from the world of the senses and rose in consciousness to that level which He desired to express.

There He remained until He became one with the consciousness to which He ascended. When He returned to the world of man, He could act with the positive assurance of that which He was conscious of being, a state of consciousness no one but Himself felt or knew that He possessed.

Man who is ignorant of this everlasting law of expression looks upon such happenings as miracles.

To rise in consciousness to the level of the thing desired and to remain there until such level becomes your nature is the way of all seeming miracles. "And I, if I be lifted up, I shall draw all men unto Me." "And I, if I be lifted up from the earth, will draw all men unto Me." [John 12:32]. If I be lifted up in consciousness to the naturalness of the thing desired, I shall draw the manifestation of that desire to me.

No man comes unto Me save the Father within Me draws him.

—John 6:44

and

I and My Father are one.

—John 10:30

My consciousness is the Father who draws the manifestation of life to me. The nature of the manifestation is determined by the state of consciousness in which I dwell. I am always drawing into my world that which I am conscious of being.

If you are dissatisfied with your present expression of life, then you must be born again [John 3:7]. Rebirth is the dropping of that level with which you are dissatisfied and rising to that level of consciousness which you desire to express and possess.

You cannot serve two masters [Matthew 6:24, Luke 16:13] or opposing states of consciousness at the same time.

Taking your attention from one state and placing it upon the other, you die to the one from which you have taken it and you live and express the one with which you are united.

Man cannot see how it would be possible to express that which he desires to be by so simple a law as acquiring the consciousness of the thing desired.

The reason for this lack of faith on the part of man is that he looks at the desired state through the consciousness of his present limitations. Therefore, he naturally sees it as impossible of accomplishment.

One of the first things man must realize is that it is impossible, in dealing with this spiritual law of consciousness, to put new wine into old bottles or new patches on old garments [Matthew 9:16,17; Mark 2:21,22; Luke 5:36-39].

That is, you cannot take any part of the present consciousness into the new state. For the state sought is complete in itself and needs no patching. Every level of consciousness automatically expresses itself.

To rise to the level of any state is to automatically become that state in expression. But, in order to rise to the level that you are not now expressing, you must completely drop the consciousness with which you are now identified.

Until your present consciousness is dropped, you will not be able to rise to another level.

Do not be dismayed. This letting go of your present identity is not as difficult as it might appear to be.

The invitation of the scriptures, "To be absent from the body and be present with the Lord" [2Corinthians 5:8, 1Corinthians 5:3, Colossians 2:5], is not given to a select few; it is a sweeping call to all mankind. The body from which you are invited to escape is your present conception of yourself with all of its limitations, while the Lord with whom you are to be present is your awareness of being.

To accomplish this seemingly impossible feat, you take your attention away from your problem and place it upon just being. You say silently but feelingly, "I AM". Do not condition this awareness but continue declaring quietly, "I AM – I AM". Simply feel that you are faceless and formless and continue doing so until you feel yourself floating.

"Floating" is a psychological state which completely denies the physical. Through practice in relaxation and willfully refusing to react to sensory impressions, it is possible to develop a state of consciousness of pure receptivity. It is a surprisingly easy accomplishment. In this state of complete detachment, a definite singleness of purposeful thought can be indelibly engraved upon your unmodified consciousness. This state of consciousness is necessary for true meditation.

This wonderful experience of rising and floating is the signal that you are absent from the body or problem and are now present with the Lord; in this expanded state you are not conscious of being anything but I AM – I AM; you are only conscious of being.

When this expansion of consciousness is attained, within this formless deep of yourself, give form to the new conception by claiming and feeling yourself to be that which you, before you entered into this state, desired to be. You will find that within this formless deep of yourself all things appear to be divinely possible. Anything that you sincerely feel yourself to be while in this expanded state becomes, in time, your natural expression.

And God said, "Let there be a firmament in the midst of the waters" [Genesis 1:6]. Yes, let there be a firmness or conviction in the midst of this expanded consciousness by knowing and feeling I AM that, the thing desired.

As you claim and feel yourself to be the thing desired, you are crystallizing this formless liquid light that you are into the image and likeness [Genesis 1:26] of that which you are conscious of being.

Now that the law of your being has been revealed to you, begin this day to change your world by revaluing yourself. Too long has man held to the belief that he is born of sorrow and must work out his salvation by the sweat of his brow. God is impersonal and no respecter of persons [Acts 10:34; Romans 2:11]. So long as man continues to walk in this belief of sorrow, so long will he walk. In a world of sorrow and confusion, for the world in its every detail is man's consciousness crystallized.

In the Book of Numbers it is recorded:

> *There were giants in the land and we were in our own sight as grasshoppers, and we were in their sight as grasshoppers.*
>
> —Numbers 13:33

Today is the day, the eternal now, when conditions in the world have attained the appearance of giants. The unemployed, the armies of the enemy, business competition etc. are the giants which make you feel yourself to be a helpless grasshopper. We are told we were first in our own sight helpless grasshoppers and because of this conception of ourselves were to the enemy helpless grasshoppers.

We can be to others only that which we are to ourselves.

Therefore, as we revalue ourselves and begin to feel ourselves to be the giant, a center of power, we automatically change our relationship to the giants, reducing these former monsters to their true place, making them appear to be the helpless grasshoppers.

Paul said of this principle, "It is to the Greeks *(or the so-called wise men of the world)* foolishness; and to the Jews *(or those who look for signs)* a stumbling block." "For the Jews require a sign, and the Greeks seek after wisdom; but we preach Christ crucified, unto the Jews a stumbling block, and unto the Greeks foolishness. But unto them which are called, both Jews and Greeks, Christ the power of God, and the wisdom of God. Because the foolishness of God is wiser than men;

and the weakness of God is stronger than men." 1Corinthians 1:22-25]. With the result that man continues to walk in darkness rather than awake to the realization:

> *I AM the light of the world.*
>
> —Matthew 5:14; John 8:12

Man has so long worshiped the images of his own making that at first he finds this revelation blasphemous, but the day man discovers and accepts this principle as the basis of his life, that day man slays his belief in a God apart from himself.

The story of Jesus' betrayal in the Garden of Gethsemane is the perfect illustration of man's discovery of this principle. We are told, the crowds armed with staves and lanterns sought Jesus in the dark of night.

As they inquired after the whereabouts of Jesus (salvation), the voice answered, "I AM"; whereupon the entire crowd fell to the ground. On regaining their composure, they again asked to be shown the hiding place of the savior and again the savior said:

> *I have told you that I AM, therefore if ye seek Me, let all else go.*
>
> —John 18:8

Man in the darkness of human ignorance sets out on his search for God, aided by the flickering light of human wisdom.

As it is revealed to man that his I AM or awareness of being is his savior, the shock is so great, he mentally falls to the ground, for every belief that he has ever entertained tumbles as he realizes that his consciousness is the one and only savior.

The knowledge that his I AM is God compels man to let all others go for he finds it impossible to serve two Gods. Man cannot accept his awareness of being as God and at the same time believe in another deity.

With this discovery, man's human ear or hearing (understanding) is cut off by the sword of faith (Peter) as his perfect disciplined hearing (understanding) is restored by (Jesus) the knowledge that I AM is Lord and Savior.

Before man can transform his world, he must first lay this foundation or understanding.

I AM the Lord [and there is none else].

—Isaiah 45:5

Man must know that his awareness of being is God.

Until this is firmly established so that no suggestion or argument of others can shake him, he will find himself returning to the slavery of his former belief.

If ye believe not that I AM He, ye shall die in your sins.

—John 8:24

Unless man discovers that his consciousness is the cause of every expression of his life, he will continue seeking the cause of his confusion in the world of effects, and so shall die in his fruitless search.

I AM the vine and ye are the branches.

—John 15:5

Consciousness is the vine and that which you are conscious of being is as branches that you feed and keep alive. Just as a branch has no life except it be rooted in the vine, likewise things have no life except you be conscious of them.

Just as a branch withers and dies if the sap of the vine ceases to flow towards it, so do things and qualities pass away if you take your attention from them; because your attention is the sap of life which sustains the expression of your life.

CHAPTER 4

Whom Seek Ye?

I have told you that I AM; if therefore ye seek Me, let these go their way.

—John 18:8

As soon then as He had said unto them, I AM, they went backward and fell to the ground.

—John 18:6

Today there is so much said about Masters, Elder Brothers, Adepts, and initiates that numberless truth seekers are being constantly misled by seeking these false lights.

For a price, most of these pseudo-teachers offer their students initiation into the mysteries, promising them guidance and direction. Man's weakness for leaders, as well as his worship of idols, makes him an easy prey of these schools and teachers.

Good will come to most of these enrolled students; they will discover after years of awaiting and sacrificing that they were following a mirage.

They will then become disillusioned in their schools and teachers, and this disappointment will be worth the effort and price they have paid for their fruitless search.

They will then turn from their worship of man and in so doing discover that which they are seeking is not to be found in another, for the Kingdom of Heaven is within [Luke 17:21].

This realization will be their first real initiation.

The lesson learned will be this: There is only one Master and this Master is God — the I AM within themselves.

I AM the Lord thy God who led thee out of the land of darkness; out of the house of bondage.

—Exodus 20:2, Deuteronomy 5:6

I AM — your awareness — is Lord and Master, and besides your awareness there is neither Lord nor Master.

You are Master of all that you will ever be aware of being.

You know that you are, do you not? Knowing that you are is the Lord and Master of that which you know that you are.

You could be completely isolated by man from that which you are conscious of being; yet you would, in spite of all human barriers, effortlessly draw to yourself all that you were conscious of being.

The man who is conscious of being poor does not need the assistance of anyone to express his poverty. The man who is conscious of being sick, though isolated in the most hermetically sealed germ-proof area in the world, would express sickness.

There is no barrier to God, for God is your awareness of being.

Regardless of what you are aware of being, you can and do express it without effort.

Stop looking for the Master to come; he is with you always.

I AM with you always, even unto the end of the world.

Matthew 28:20

You will from time to time know yourself to be many things, but you need not be anything to know that you are.

You can, if you so desire, disentangle yourself from the body you wear; in so doing, you realize that you are a faceless, formless awareness and not dependent on the form you are in your expression.

You will know that you are; you will also discover that this "knowing that you are" is God, the Father, which preceded all that you ever knew yourself to be.

Before the world was, you were aware of being, and so you were saying "I AM", and I AM will be; after all that you know yourself to be shall cease to be.

There are no Ascended Masters. Banish this superstition.

You will forever rise from one level of consciousness (master) to another; in so doing, you manifest the ascended level, expressing this newly acquired consciousness.

Consciousness being Lord and Master, you are the Master Magician conjuring that which you are now conscious of being.

> *For God (consciousness) calleth those things which be not as though they were.*
>
> —Romans 4:17

Things that are not now seen will be seen the moment you become conscious of being that which is not now seen.

This rising from one level of consciousness to another is the only ascension that you will ever experience.

No man can lift you to the level you desire. The power to ascend is within yourself; it is your consciousness.

You appropriate the consciousness of the level you desire to express by claiming that you are now expressing such a level.

This is the ascension. It is limitless, for you will never exhaust your capacity to ascend.

Turn from the human superstition of ascension with its belief in masters, and find the only and everlasting master within yourself.

> *Far greater is he that is in you than he that is in the world.*
>
> —1 John 4:4

Believe this.

Do not continue in blindness, following after the mirage of masters. I assure you your search can end only in disappointment.

> *If you deny Me (your awareness of being), I shall deny you also.*
>
> —Matthew 10:33

Thou shalt have no other God beside ME.

—Isaiah 45:5; Joel 2:27

Be still and know that I AM God.

—Psalm 46:10

Come prove me and see if I will not open you the windows of Heaven and pour you out a blessing, that there shall not be room enough to receive it.

—Malachi 3:10

Do you believe that the I AM is able to do this?

Then claim ME to be that which you want to see poured out.

Claim yourself to be that which you want to be and that you shall be.

Not because of masters will I give it unto you, but because you have recognized ME (yourself) to be that, I will give it unto you, for I AM all things to all.

Jesus would not permit Himself to be called Good Master. He knew that there is but one good and one master. He knew this one to be His Father in Heaven, the awareness of being. "The Kingdom of God" (Good) and the Kingdom of Heaven are within you [Luke 17:21].

Your belief in masters is a confession of your slavery. Only slaves have masters.

Change your conception of yourself and you will, without the aid of masters or anyone else, automatically transform your world to conform to your changed conception of yourself.

You are told in the Book of Numbers that there was a time when men were in their own eyes as grasshoppers and because of this conception of themselves, they saw giants in the land. This is as true of man today as it was the day it was recorded. Man's conception of himself is so grasshopper-like, that he automatically makes the conditions round about him appear gigantic; in his blindness he cries out for masters to help him fight his giant problems.

Jesus tried to show man that salvation was within himself and warned him not to look for his savior in places or people.

> *If anyone should come saying look here or look there, believe him not, for the Kingdom of Heaven is within you.*
>
> —Luke 17:21

Jesus not only refused to permit Himself to be called Good Master, He warned his followers, "Salute no man along the highway," "and greet no man along the way" [Luke 10:4; 2Kings 4:29]. He made it clear that they should not recognize any authority or superior other than God, the Father.

Jesus established the identity of the Father as man's awareness of being. "I and My Father are one, but My Father is greater than I" [John 10:30, John 14:28]. I AM one with all that I am conscious of being. I AM greater than that which I am aware of being. The creator is ever greater than his creation.

"As Moses lifted up the serpent in the wilderness even so must the Son of Man be lifted up" [John 3:14]. The serpent symbolizes man's present conception of himself as a worm of the dust, living in the wilderness of human confusion. Just as Moses lifted himself from his worm-of-the-dust conception of himself to discover God to be his awareness of being, "I AM hath sent me" [Exodus 3:14], so must you be lifted up. The day you claim, as did Moses, "I AM that I AM" [Exodus 3:14], that day your claim will blossom in the wilderness.

Your awareness is the master magician who conjures all things by being that which he would conjure. This Lord and Master that you are can and does make all that you are conscious of being appear in your world.

"No man *(manifestation)* cometh unto Me save My Father draw him and I and My Father are one."

> *No man can come to Me, except the Father which hath sent Me draw him: and I will raise him up at the last day.*
>
> —John 6:44]

> *My Father, which gave them Me, is greater than all; and no man is able to pluck them out of My Father's hand. I and My Father are one.*
>
> —John 10:29, 30

You are constantly drawing to yourself that which you are conscious of being. Change your conception of yourself from that of the slave to that of Christ.

Don't be embarrassed to make this claim; only as you claim, "I AM Christ", will you do the works of Christ.

"The works I do ye shall do also, and greater works than these shall ye do, for I go unto my Father."

> *Truly, truly, I say to you, he who believes in Me, the works that I do, he will do also; and greater works than these he will do; because I go to the Father.*
>
> —John 14:12

> *He made Himself equal with God and found it not robbery to do the works of God.*
>
> —Philippians 2:6

Jesus knew that anyone who dared to claim himself to be Christ would automatically assume the capacities to express the works of his conception of Christ.

Jesus also knew that the exclusive use of this principle of expression was not given to Him alone.

He constantly referred to His Father in Heaven.

He stated that His works would not only be equaled but that they would be surpassed by that man who dared to conceive himself to be greater than He (Jesus) had conceived Himself to be.

Jesus, in stating that He and His Father were one but that His Father was greater than He, revealed His awareness (Father) to be one with that which He was aware of being.

He found Himself as Father or awareness to be greater than that which He as Jesus was aware of being.

You and your conception of yourself are one.

You are and always will be greater than any conception you will ever have of yourself.

Man fails to do the works of Jesus Christ because he attempts to accomplish them from his present level of consciousness.

You will never transcend your present accomplishments through sacrifice and struggle.

Your present level of consciousness will only be transcended as you drop the present state and rise to a higher level.

You rise to a higher level of consciousness by taking your attention away from your present limitations and placing it upon that which you desire to be. Do not attempt this in day-dreaming or wishful thinking, but in a positive manner.

Claim yourself to be the thing desired. I AM that; no sacrifice, no diet, no human tricks.

All that is asked of you is to accept your desire. If you dare claim it, you will express it.

Meditate on these:

I rejoice not in the sacrifices of men.

—(probably) Malachi 1:10

Not by might nor by power, but by my spirit.

—Zechariah 4:6

Ask and you shall receive.

—Matthew 7:7, Matthew 21:22, Mark 11:24,
Luke 11:9, John 15:7, John 16:24

Come eat and drink without price.

—(probably) Isaiah 55:1

The works are finished. All that is required of you to let these qualities into expression is the claim – I AM that. Claim yourself to be that which you desire to be and that you shall be.

Expressions follow the impressions, they do not precede them. Proof that you are will follow the claim that you are, it will not precede it.

"Leave all and follow Me" [Matthew 8:22; 9:9; Luke 5:27] is a double invitation to you.

First, it invites you to turn completely away from all problems and, then, it calls upon you to continue walking in the claim that you are that which you desire to be.

Do not be a Lot's wife who looks back and becomes salted [Genesis 19] or preserved in the dead past.

Be a Lot who does not look back but who keeps his vision focused upon the promised land, the thing desired.

Do this and you will know that you have found the master, the Master Magician, making the unseen the seen through the command, "I AM THAT".

CHAPTER 5

Who Am I?

But whom say ye that I AM?

—Matt. 16:15

I AM the Lord; that is My name; and My glory will I not give to another.

—Isaiah 42:8

I AM the Lord, the God of all Flesh.

—Jeremiah 32:27

This I AM within you, the reader, this awareness, this consciousness of being, is the Lord, the God of all Flesh.

I AM is He that should come; stop looking for another. As long as you believe in a God apart from yourself, you will continue to transfer the power of your expression to your conceptions, forgetting that you are the conceiver.

The power conceiving and the thing conceived are one but the power to conceive is greater than the conception.

Jesus discovered this glorious truth when He declared:

I and My Father are one, but My Father is greater than I.

—John 10:30, John 14:28

The power conceiving itself to be man is greater than its conception. All conceptions are limitations of the conceiver.

Before Abraham was, I AM.

—John 8:58

Before the world was, I AM.

Consciousness precedes all manifestations and is the prop upon which all manifestation rests.

To remove the manifestations, all that is required of you, the conceiver, is to take your attention away from the conception. Instead of "Out of sight, out of mind", it really is "Out of mind, out of sight".

The manifestation will remain in sight only as long as it takes the force with which the conceiver – I AM – originally endowed it to spend itself. This applies to all creation from the infinitesimally small electron to the infinitely great universe.

Be still and know that I AM God.

—Psalm 46:10

Yes, this very I AM, your awareness of being, is God, the only God. I AM is the Lord – the God of all Flesh – all manifestation.

This presence, your unconditioned awareness, comprehends neither beginning nor ending; limitations exist only in the manifestation. When you realize that this awareness is your eternal self, you will know that before Abraham was, I AM.

Begin to understand why you were told:

Go thou and do likewise.

—Luke 10:37

Begin now to identify yourself with this presence, your awareness, as the only reality.

All manifestations but appear to be; you as man have no reality other than that which your eternal self, I AM, believes itself to be.

Whom do you say that I AM?

—Matthew 16:15, Mark 8:29, Luke 9:20

This is not a question asked two thousand years ago. It is the eternal question addressed to the manifestation by the conceiver.

It is your true self, your awareness of being, asking you, its present conception of itself, "Who do you believe your awareness to be?"

This answer can be defined only within yourself, regardless of the influence of another.

I AM *(your true self)* is not interested in man's opinion.

All its interest lies in your conviction of yourself.

What do you say of the I AM within you? Can you answer and say, "I AM Christ"?

Your answer or degree of understanding will determine the place you will occupy in life.

Do you say or believe yourself to be a man of a certain family race, nation, etc.? Do you honestly believe this of yourself?

Then life, your true self will cause these conceptions to appear in your world and you will live with them as though they are real.

I AM the door.

—John 10:9

I AM the way.

—John 14:6

I AM the resurrection and the life.

—John 11:25

No man (or manifestation) cometh unto My Father save by Me.
I am the way, the truth, and the life: no man cometh unto the Father, but by Me.

—John 14:6

The I AM *(your consciousness)* is the only door through which anything can pass into your world.

Stop looking for signs. Signs follow; they do not precede. Begin to reverse the statement, "Seeing is believing", to "Believing is seeing". Start now to believe, not with the wavering confidence based on deceptive external evidence but with an undaunted confidence based on the immutable law that you can be that which you desire to be. You will find that you are not a victim of fate but a victim of faith *(your own)*.

Only through one door can that which you seek pass into the world of manifestation. "I AM the door". Your consciousness is the door, so you must become conscious of being and having that which you desire to be and to have. Any attempt to realize your desires in ways other than through the door of consciousness makes you a thief and a robber unto yourself.

Any expression that is not felt is unnatural. Before anything appears, God, I AM, feels itself to be the thing desired; and then the thing felt appears. It is resurrected; lifted out of the nothingness.

I AM wealthy, poor, healthy, sick, free, confined, were first of all impressions or conditions felt before they became visible expressions.

Your world is your consciousness objectified. Waste no time trying to change the outside; change the within or the impression; and the without or expression will take care of itself.

When the truth of this statement dawns upon you, you will know that you have found the lost word or the key to every door.

I AM *(your consciousness)* is the magical lost word which was made flesh in the likeness of that which you are conscious of being.

I AM He. Right now, I am overshadowing you, the reader, my living temple, with my presence, urging upon you a new expression. Your desires are my spoken words. My words are spirit and they are true and they shall not return unto me void but shall accomplish where unto they are sent.

> *So shall my word be that goeth forth out of my mouth: it shall not return unto me void, but it shall accomplish that which I please, and it shall prosper in the thing whereto I sent it.*
>
> —Isaiah 55:11

They are not something to be worked out.

They are garments that I, your faceless, formless self, wear. Behold! I, clothed in your desire, stand at the door (*your consciousness)* and knock. If you hear my voice and open unto me *(recognize me as your savior)*, I will come in unto you and sup with you and you with me.

> *Behold, I stand at the door, and knock: if any man hear my voice, and open the door, I will come in to him, and will sup with him, and he with me.*
>
> —Revelation 3:20

Just how my words, your desires, will be fulfilled, is not your concern. My words have a way ye know not of [John 4:32]. Their ways are past finding out [Romans 11:33].

All that is required of you is to believe. Believe your desires to be garments your savior wears. Your belief that you are now that which you desire to be is proof of your acceptance of life's gifts. You have opened the door for your Lord, clothed in your desire, to enter the moment you establish this belief.

> *When ye pray, believe that ye have received and it shall be so.*
>
> —Mark 11:24

> *All things are possible to him who believes.*
>
> —Mark 9:23

Make the impossible possible through your belief; and the impossible *(to others)* will embody itself in your world.

All men have had proof of the power of faith. The faith that moves mountains is faith in yourself.

No man has faith in God who lacks confidence in himself. Your faith in God is measured by your confidence in yourself. "I and My Father are one" [John 10:30]; man and his God are one, consciousness and manifestation are one.

And God said, "Let there be a firmament in the midst of the waters" [Genesis 1:6]. In the midst of all the doubts and changing opinions of others, let there be a conviction, a firmness of belief, and you shall see the dry land; your belief will appear.

The reward is to him that endureth unto the end: "But he that shall endure unto the end, the same shall be saved" [Matthew 24:13]. A conviction is not a conviction if it can be shaken. Your desire will be as clouds without rain unless you believe.

Your unconditioned awareness or I AM is the Virgin Mary who knew not a man [Luke 1:34], and yet, unaided by man, conceived and bore a son. Mary, the unconditioned consciousness, desired and then became conscious of being the conditioned state which she desired to express, and in a way unknown to others, became it. Go and do likewise; assume the consciousness of that which you desire to be and you, too, will give birth to your savior.

When the annunciation is made, when the urge or desire is upon you, believe it to be God's spoken word seeking embodiment through you. Go, tell no man of this holy thing that you have conceived. Lock your secret within you and magnify the Lord [Luke 1:46] — magnify or believe your desire to be your savior coming to be with you.

When this belief is so firmly established that you feel confident of results, your desire will embody itself. How it will be done, no man knows. I, your desire, have ways ye know not of [John 4:32]. My ways are past finding out [Romans 11:33]. Your desire can be likened to a seed, and seeds contain within themselves both the power and the plan of self-expression. Your consciousness is the soil. These seeds are successfully planted only if, after you have claimed yourself to be and to have that which you desire, you confidently await results without an anxious thought.

If I be lifted up in consciousness to the naturalness of my desire, I shall automatically draw the manifestation unto me.

Consciousness is the door through which life reveals itself. Consciousness is always objectifying itself.

To be conscious of being or possessing anything is to be or have that which you are conscious of being or possessing. Therefore, lift yourself to the consciousness of your desire and you will see it automatically out-picture itself.

To do this, you must deny your present identity. "Let him deny himself" [Mark 8:34]. You deny a thing by taking your attention away from it. To drop a thing, problem or ego from consciousness, you dwell upon God – God being I AM. Be still and know that I AM is God [Psalm 46:10].

Believe, feel that I AM; know that this knowing one within you, your awareness of being, is God.

Close your eyes and feel yourself to be faceless, formless and without figure. Approach this stillness as though it were the easiest thing in the world to accomplish. This attitude will assure your success.

When all thought of problem or self is dropped from consciousness because you are now absorbed or lost in the feeling of just being I AM, then begin in this formless state to feel yourself to be that which you desire to be, "I AM that I AM".

The moment you reach a certain degree of intensity so that you actually feel yourself to be a new conception, this new feeling or consciousness is established and in due time will personify itself in the world of form.

This new perception will express itself as naturally as you now express your present identity.

To express the qualities of a consciousness naturally, you must dwell or live within that consciousness. Appropriate it by becoming one with it. To feel a thing intensely, and then rest confidently that it is, makes the thing felt appear within your world.

"I shall stand upon my watch" [Habakkuk 2:1] "and see the salvation of the Lord" [2Chronicles 20:17]. I shall stand firmly upon my feeling, convinced that it is so, and see my desire appear.

> *A man can receive nothing (no thing) except it be given him from Heaven.*
>
> —John 3:27

Remember, heaven is your consciousness; the Kingdom of Heaven is within you.

This is why you are warned against calling any man Father; your consciousness is the Father of all that you are.

Again you are told, "Salute no man on the highway" [Luke 10:4; 2Kings 4:29]. See no man as an authority. Why should you ask man for permission to express when you realize that your world, in its every detail, originated within you and is sustained by you as the only conceptional center?

Your whole world may be likened to solidified space mirroring the beliefs and acceptances as projected by a formless, faceless presence, namely, I AM. Reduce the whole to its primordial substance and nothing would remain but you, a dimensionless presence, the conceiver.

The conceiver is a law apart. Conceptions under such law are not to be measured by past accomplishments or modified by present capacities for, without taking thought, the conception in a way unknown to man expresses itself.

Go within secretly and appropriate the new consciousness. Feel yourself to be it, and the former limitations shall pass away as completely and as easily as snow on a hot summer's day.

You will not even remember the former limitations; they were never part of this new consciousness.

This rebirth Jesus referred to when he said to Nicodemus, "Ye must be born again" [John 3:7], was nothing more than moving from one state of consciousness to another.

Whatsoever ye shall ask in My name, that will I do.

—John 14:13; similarly, John 15:16; John 16:23

This certainly does not mean to ask in words, pronouncing with the lips the sounds, God or Christ Jesus, for millions have asked in this manner without results.

To feel yourself to be a thing is to have asked for that thing in His name. I AM is the nameless presence. To feel yourself to be rich is to ask for wealth in His name.

I AM is unconditioned. It is neither rich nor poor, strong nor weak. In other words, in HIM there is neither Greek nor Jew, bond nor free, male nor female. These are all conceptions or limitations of the limitless, and therefore names of the nameless.

To feel yourself to be anything is to ask the nameless, I AM, to express that name or nature".

> *Ask whatsoever ye will in My name by appropriating the nature of the thing desired and I will give it unto you.*

CHAPTER 6

I Am He

For if ye believe not that I AM, ye shall die in your sins.

—John 8:24.

All things were made by Him; and without Him was not anything made that was made.

—John 1:3

This is a hard saying for those trained in the various systems of orthodox religion to accept, but there it stands.

All things, good, bad and indifferent, were made by God.

God made man (manifestation) in His own image; in the likeness of God made He him.

—Genesis 1:27

Apparently adding to this confusion, it is stated:

And God saw that his creation was good.

—Genesis 1:31

What are you going to do about this seeming anomaly? How is man going to correlate all things as good when that which he is taught denies this fact?

Either the understanding of God is erroneous or else there is something radically wrong with man's teaching.

To the pure all things are pure.

—Titus 1:15

This is another puzzling statement. All the good people, the pure people, the holy people, are the greatest prohibitionists. Couple the foregoing statement with this one, "There is no condemnation in Christ Jesus", and you get an impassable barrier to the self-appointed judges of the world.

There is therefore now no condemnation to them which are in Christ Jesus, who walk not after the flesh, but after the Spirit.

—Romans 8:1

Such statements mean nothing to the self-righteous judges blindly changing and destroying shadows. They continue in the firm belief that they are improving the world.

Man, not knowing that his world is his individual consciousness out-pictured, vainly strives to conform to the opinion of others rather than to conform to the one and only opinion existent, namely, his own judgment of himself.

When Jesus discovered His consciousness to be this wonderful law of self-government, He declared, "And now I sanctify Myself that they also might be sanctified through the truth."

And for their sakes I sanctify Myself, that they also might be sanctified through the truth.

—John 17:19

He knew that consciousness was the only reality, that things objectified were nothing more than different states of consciousness.

Jesus warned His followers to seek first the Kingdom of Heaven (that state of consciousness that would produce the thing desired) and all things would be added to them [Matthew 6:33].

He also stated,

I AM the truth.

—John 14:6

He knew that man's consciousness was the truth or cause of all that man saw his world to be. Jesus realized that the world was made in the likeness of man. He knew that man saw his world to be what it was because man was what he was.

In short, man's conception of himself determines that which he sees his world to be.

All things are made by God (consciousness) and without him there is nothing made that is made.

—John 1:3

Creation is judged good and very good because it is the perfect likeness of that consciousness which produced it.

To be conscious of being one thing and then see yourself expressing something other than that which you are conscious of being is a violation of the law of being; therefore, it would not be good. The law of being is never broken; man ever sees himself expressing that which he is conscious of being.

Be it good, bad or indifferent, it is nevertheless a perfect likeness of his conception of himself; it is good and very good.

Not only are all things made by God, all things are made of God. All are the offspring of God. God is one. Things or divisions are the projections of the one. God being one, He must command Himself to be the seeming other, for there is no other.

The absolute cannot contain something within itself that is not itself. If it did, then it would not be absolute, the only one.

Commands, to be effective, must be to oneself. "I AM that I AM" is the only effective command.

I AM the Lord and beside Me there is none else.

—Isaiah 45:5; Joel 2:27

You cannot command that which is not. As there is no other, you must command yourself to be that which you would have appear.

Let me clarify what I mean by effective command. You do not repeat like a parrot the statement, "I AM that I AM"; such vain repetition would be both stupid and fruitless.

It is not the words that make it effective; it is the consciousness of being the thing which makes it effective.

When you say, "I AM", you are declaring yourself to be. The word that in the statement, "I AM that I AM", indicates that which you would be. The second "I AM" in the quotation is the cry of victory.

This whole drama takes place inwardly with or without the use of words.

Be still and know that you are.

This stillness is attained by observing the observer.

Repeat quietly but with feeling, "I AM – I AM", until you have lost all consciousness of the world and know yourself just as being.

Awareness, the knowing that you are, is Almighty God — I AM.

After this is accomplished, define yourself as that which you desire to be by feeling yourself to be the thing desired: I AM *that*. This understanding that you are the thing desired will cause a thrill to course through your entire being. When the conviction is established and you really believe that you are that which you desired to be, then the second "I AM" is uttered as a cry of victory. This mystical revelation of Moses can be seen as three distinct steps: I AM; I AM free; I really AM!

It does not matter what the appearances round about you are like. All things make way for the coming of the Lord. I AM the Lord coming in the appearance of that which I am conscious of being. All the inhabitants of the earth cannot stay my coming or question my authority to be that which I AM conscious that I AM .

> *All the inhabitants of the earth are as nothing, and He doeth according to His will in the armies of Heaven and among all the inhabitants of the earth; and none can stay His hand, nor say unto Him, 'What doest Thou?'*
>
> —Daniel 4:35

"I AM the light of the world" [John 8:12], crystallizing into the form of my conception of myself.

Consciousness is the eternal light, which crystallizes only through the medium of your conception of yourself.

Change your conception of yourself and you will automatically change the world in which you live. Do not try to change people; they are only messengers telling you who you are. Revalue yourself and they will confirm the change.

Now you will realize why Jesus sanctified Himself instead of others [John 17:19], why to the pure all things are pure [Titus 1:15], why in Christ Jesus (the awakened consciousness) there is no condemnation [Romans 8:1].

Awake from the sleep of condemnation and prove the principle of life. Stop not only your judgment of others but your condemnation of yourself.

Hear the revelation of the enlightened:

> *I know and am persuaded by the Lord Christ Jesus that there is nothing unclean of itself, but to him that seeth anything to be unclean to him it is unclean.*
>
> —Romans 14:14

And again,

> *Happy is the man who condemneth himself not in that which he alloweth.*
>
> *Happy is he that condemneth not himself in that thing which he alloweth.*
>
> —Romans 14:22

Stop asking yourself whether or not you are worthy or unworthy to claim yourself to be that which you desire to be. You will be condemned by the world only as long as you condemn yourself.

You do not need to work out anything. The works are finished. The principle by which all things are made and without which there is not anything made that is made is eternal. You are this principle.

Your awareness of being is this everlasting law. You have never expressed anything that you were not aware of being and you never will. Assume the consciousness of that which you desire to express. Claim it until it becomes a natural manifestation. Feel it and live within that feeling until you make it your nature.

Here is a simple formula. Take your attention from your present conception of yourself and place it on that ideal of yours, the ideal you had heretofore thought beyond your reach. Claim yourself to be your ideal, not as something that you will be in time, but as that which you are in the immediate present.

Do this, and your present world of limitations will disintegrate as your new claim rises like the phoenix from its ashes.

> *Be not afraid nor dismayed by reason of this great multitude; for the battle is not yours, but God's.*
>
> —2 Chronicles 20:15

You do not fight against your problem; your problem will only live as long as you are conscious of it. Take your attention away from your problem and the multitude of reasons why you cannot achieve your ideal. Concentrate your attention entirely upon the thing desired.

> *Leave all and follow me*
>
> —Matthew 8:22; 9:9; Luke 5:27

In the face of seemingly mountainous obstacles, claim your freedom. The consciousness of freedom is the Father of freedom. It has a way of expressing itself which no man knows.

> *Ye shall not need to fight in this battle. Set yourself, stand still, and see the salvation of the Lord with you*
>
> —2 Chronicles 20:17

"I AM the Lord." I AM (your consciousness) is the Lord. The consciousness that the thing is done, that the work is finished, is the Lord of any situation.

Listen carefully to the promise,

> *Ye shall not need to fight in this battle. Set yourself, stand still, and see the salvation of the Lord with you.*
>
> —2 Chronicles 20:17

With you!

That particular consciousness with which you are identified is the Lord of the agreement. He will without assistance establish the thing agreed upon on earth.

Can you, in the face of the army of reasons why a thing cannot be done, quietly enter into an agreement with the Lord that it is done?

Can you, now that you have found the Lord to be your awareness of being, become aware that the battle is won?

Can you, no matter how near and threatening the enemy seems to be, continue in your confidence, standing still, knowing that the victory is yours?

If you can, you will see the salvation of the Lord. Remember, the reward is to the one who endures [Matthew 24:13].

> *Stand still.*
>
> —Psalm 46:10

Standing still is the deep conviction that all is well; it is done. No matter what is heard or seen, you remain unmoved, conscious of being victorious in the end.

All things are made by such agreements, and without such an agreement, there is not anything made that is made [John 1:3].

> *I AM that I AM.*
>
> —Exodus 3:14

In Revelations, it is recorded that a new heaven and new earth shall appear [21:1].

John, shown this vision, was told to write, "It is done" [21:6].

Heaven is your consciousness, and earth its solidified state. Therefore, accept as did John – "It is done".

All that is required of you who seek a change is to rise to a level of that which you desire; without dwelling upon the manner of expression, record that it is done by feeling the naturalness of being it.

Here is an analogy that might help you to see this mystery.

Suppose you entered a motion-picture theatre just as the feature picture came to its end. All that you saw of the picture was the happy-ending. Because you wanted to see the entire story, you waited for it to unfold again. With the anti-climactic sequence, the hero is displayed as accused, surrounded by false evidence, and all that goes to wring tears from the audience. But you, secure in the knowledge of the ending, remain calm with the understanding that, regardless of the seeming direction of the picture, the end has already been defined.

In like manner, go to the end of that which you seek; witness the happy end of it by consciously feeling you express and possess that which you desire to express and possess; and you, through faith, already understanding the end, will have confidence born of this knowledge.

This knowledge will sustain you through the necessary interval of time that it takes the picture to unfold.

Ask no help of man. Feel "It is done" by consciously claiming yourself to be now that which as man you hope to be.

CHAPTER 7

Thy Will Be Done

Not My will, but Thine, be done.

—Luke 22:42

O My Father, if this cup may not pass away from Me, except I drink it, Thy will be done.

—Matthew 26:42

Nevertheless not what I will, but what Thou wilt.

—Mark 14:36

This resignation is not one of blind realization that "I can of Myself do nothing, the Father within Me, He doeth the work."

I can of Mine own Self do nothing; as I hear, I judge, and My judgment is just because I seek not Mine own will, but the will of the Father which hath sent Me.

—John 5:30

Believest thou not that I am in the Father, and the Father in Me? The words that I speak unto you I speak not of Myself; but the Father that dwelleth in Me, He doeth the works.

—John 14:10

When man wills, he attempts to make something which does not now exist appear in time and space.

Too often we are not aware of that which we are really doing. We unconsciously state that we do not possess the capacities to express. We predicate our desire upon the hope of acquiring the necessary capacities in future time. "I AM not, but I will be".

Man does not realize that consciousness is the Father which does the work, so he attempts to express that which he is not conscious of being.

Such struggles are doomed to failure; only the present expresses itself. Unless I am conscious of being that which I seek, I will not find it. God (your awareness) is the substance and fullness of all.

God's will is the recognition of that which *is*, not of that which *will be*.

Instead of seeing this saying as "Thine will be done", see it as "Thy will is done". The works are finished.

The principle by which all things are made visible is eternal.

"Eyes have not seen nor ears heard, neither hath it entered into the hearts of men, the things which God hath prepared for those who love the law"

> *Eye hath not seen nor ear heard, neither hath entered into the heart of man, the things which God hath prepared for them that love Him.*
>
> —1 Corinthians 2:9-10

When a sculptor looks at a formless piece of marble he sees, buried within its formless mass, his finished piece of art. The sculptor, instead of making his masterpiece, merely reveals it by removing that part of the marble which hides his conception.

The same applies to you. In your formless awareness lies buried all that you will ever conceive yourself to be.

The recognition of this truth will transform you from an unskilled laborer who tries to make it so to a great artist who recognizes it to be so.

Your claim that you are now that which you want to be will remove the veil of human darkness and reveal your claim perfectly; I AM that.

God's will was expressed in the words of the Widow, "It is well". Man's will would have been, "It will be well". To state, "I shall be well", is to say, "I am ill".

God, the Eternal Now, is not mocked by words or vain repetition.

God continually personifies that which is.

Thus, the resignation of Jesus (who made Himself equal with God) was turning from the recognition of lack (which the future indicates with "I shall be") to the recognition of supply by claiming, "I AM that; it is done; thank You, Father".

Now you will see the wisdom in the words of the prophet when he states:

Let the weak say, I AM strong.

—Joel 3:10.

Man in his blindness will not heed the prophet's advice; he continues to claim himself to be weak, poor, wretched and all the other undesirable expressions from which he is trying to free himself by ignorantly claiming that he will be free from these characteristics in the expectancy of the future.

Such thoughts thwart the one law that can ever free him.

There is only one door through which that which you seek can enter your world. "I AM the door" [John 10:9].

When you say, "I AM", you are declaring yourself to be, first person, present tense; there is no future.

To know that I AM is to be conscious of being. Consciousness is the only door. Unless you are conscious of being that which you seek, you seek in vain.

If you judge after appearances, you will continue to be enslaved by the evidence of your senses.

To break this hypnotic spell of the senses, you are told, "Go within and shut the door"

But thou, when thou prayest, enter into thy closet, and when thou hast shut thy door, pray to thy Father which is in secret; and thy Father which seeth in secret shall reward thee openly.

—Matthew 6:6

Enter thou into thy chambers, and shut thy doors about thee: hide thyself as it were for a little moment, until the indignation be overpast.

—Isaiah 26:20

And when thou art come in, thou shalt shut the door upon thee and upon thy sons.

—2 Kings 4:4

He went in therefore, and shut the door upon them twain, and prayed unto the Lord.

—2 Kings 4:33

The door of the senses must be tightly shut before your new claim can be honored.

Closing the door of the senses is not as difficult as it appears to be at first. It is done without effort.

It is impossible to serve two masters at the same time [Matthew 6:24, Luke 16:13].

The master man serves is that which he is conscious of being. I am Lord and Master of that which I am conscious of being.

It is no effort for me to conjure poverty if I am conscious of being poor.

My servant (poverty) is compelled to follow me (conscious of poverty) as long as I AM (the Lord) conscious of being poor.

Instead of fighting against the evidence of the senses, you claim yourself to be that which you desire to be.

As your attention is placed on this claim, the doors of the senses automatically close against your former master (that which you were conscious of being).

As you become lost in the feeling of being (that which you are now claiming to be true of yourself), the doors of the senses once more open, revealing your world to be the perfect expression of that which you are conscious of being.

Let us follow the example of Jesus who realized, as man, He could do nothing to change His present picture of lack.

He closed the door of His senses against His problem and went to His Father, the one to Whom all things are possible [Matthew 19:26; Mark 9:23; 10:27; 14:36; Luke 18:27; Acts 8:37].

Having denied the evidence of His senses, He claimed Himself to be all that, a moment before, His senses told him He was not.

Knowing that consciousness expresses its likeness on earth, He remained in the claimed consciousness until the doors (His senses) opened and confirmed the rulership of the Lord.

Remember, I AM is Lord of all. Never again use the will of man which claims, "I will be". Be as resigned as Jesus and claim, "I AM that".

CHAPTER 8

No Other God

I am the first, and I am the last; and beside Me is no God.

—Isaiah 44:6

I am the Lord thy God, which brought thee out of the land of Egypt, from the house of bondage. Thou shalt have none other gods before Me.

—Deut. 5:6,7

"Thou shalt have no other God beside Me." As long as man entertains a belief in a power apart from himself, so long will he rob himself of the being that he is.

Every belief in powers apart from himself, whether for good or evil, will become the mould of the graven image worshipped.

The beliefs in the potency of drugs to heal, diets to strengthen, moneys to secure, are the values or money changers that must be thrown out of the power [Matthew 21:12; Mark 11:15; Luke 19:45; John 2:14,15] he can then unfailingly manifest that quality.

This understanding throws out the money changers Temple.

Ye are the Temple of the Living God.

—1 Corinthians 3:16; 6:19

And what agreement hath the temple of God with idols? For ye are the temple of the living God. As God hath said, 'I will dwell in them, and walk in them; and I will be their God, and they shall be my people.'

—2 Corinthians 6:16

A temple made without hands.
It is written:

My house shall be called of all nations a house of prayer, but ye have made it a den of thieves.

—Matthew 21:13

...for Mine house shall be called an house of prayer for all people.

—Isaiah 56:7

The thieves who rob you are your own false beliefs. It is your belief in a thing, not the thing itself, that aids you. There is only one power: I AM He. Because of your belief in external things, you think power into them by transferring the power that you are to the external thing. Realize you yourself are the power you have mistakenly given to outer conditions.

The Bible compares the opinionated man to the camel who could not go through the needle's eye [Matthew 19:24; Mark 10:25; Luke 18:25]. The needle's eye referred to was a small gate in the walls of Jerusalem, which was so narrow that a camel could not go through it until relieved of its pack.

The rich man, that is the one burdened with false human concepts, cannot enter the Kingdom of Heaven until relieved of his burden any more than could the camel go through this small gate [Matthew 19:23].

Man feels so secure in his man-made laws, opinions, and beliefs that he invests them with an authority they do not possess.

Satisfied that his knowledge is all, he remains unaware that all outward appearances are but states of mind externalized.

When he realizes that the consciousness of a quality externalizes that quality without the aid of any other or many values and establishes the one true value, his own consciousness.

> *The Lord is in His holy temple.*
>
> —Habakkuk 2:20

Consciousness dwells within that which it is conscious of being. I AM is the Lord and man, his temple.

Knowing that consciousness objectifies itself, man must forgive all men for being that which they are. He must realize that all are expressing (without the aid of another) that which they are conscious of being.

Peter, the enlightened or disciplined man, knew that a change of consciousness would produce a change of expression. Instead of sympathizing with the beggars of life at the temple's gate, he declared:

> *Silver and gold have I none (for thee), but such as I have (the consciousness of freedom), give I unto thee*
>
> —Acts 3:6

> *Stir up the gift within you.*

> *Wherefore I put thee in remembrance that thou stir up the gift of God, which is in thee.*
>
> —2 Timothy 1:6

Stop begging and claim yourself to be that which you decide to be. Do this and you too will jump from your crippled world into the world of freedom, singing praises to the Lord, I AM. "Far greater is He that is in you than he that is in the world."

> *Ye are of God, little children, and have overcome them: because greater is He that is in you, than he that is in the world.*
>
> —1 John 4:4

This is the cry of everyone who finds his awareness of being to be God.

Your recognition of this fact will automatically cleanse the temple, your consciousness, of the thieves and robbers, restoring to you that dominion over things, which you lost the moment you forgot the command:

Thou shalt have no other God beside ME.

CHAPTER 9

The Foundation Stone

Let every man take heed how he buildeth thereon. For other foundations can no man lay than that is laid, which is Jesus Christ. Now if man build upon this foundation gold, silver, precious stones, wood, hay, stubble; every man's work shall be made manifest; for the day shall declare it.

—1 Cor. 3:10-13

The foundation of all expression is consciousness. Try as man will, he cannot find a cause of manifestation other than his consciousness of being.

Man thinks he has found the cause of disease in germs, the cause of war in conflicting political ideologies and greed. All such discoveries of man, catalogued as the essence of Wisdom, are foolishness in the eyes of God.

There is only one power and this power is God (consciousness). It kills; it makes alive; it wounds; it heals; it does all things, good, bad or indifferent.

Man moves in a world that is nothing more or less than his consciousness objectified. Not knowing this, he wars against his reflections while he keeps alive the light and the images which project the reflections.

I AM the light of the world.

—John 8:12

I AM (consciousness) is the light.

That which I am conscious of being (my conception of myself) – such as "I am rich", "I am healthy", "I am free" – are the images.

The world is the mirror magnifying all that I AM conscious of being.

Stop trying to change the world since it is only the mirror. Man's attempt to change the world by force is as fruitless as breaking a mirror in the hope of changing his face. Leave the mirror and change your face. Leave the world alone and change your conceptions of yourself. The reflection then will be satisfactory.

Freedom or imprisonment, satisfaction or frustration, can only be differentiated by the consciousness of being.

Regardless of your problem, its duration or its magnitude, careful attention to these instructions will in an amazingly short time eliminate even the memory of the problem.

Ask yourself this question: "How would I feel if I were free?" The very moment you sincerely ask this question, the answer comes.

No man can tell another the satisfaction of his desire fulfilled. It remains for each within himself to experience the feeling and joy of this automatic change of consciousness.

The feeling or thrill that comes to one in response to his self-questioning is the Father state of consciousness or Foundation Stone upon which the conscious change is built.

Just how this feeling will embody itself no one knows, but it will. The Father (consciousness) has ways that no man knows [Romans 11:33]; it is the unalterable law. All things express their nature. As you wear a feeling, it becomes your nature.

It might take a moment or a year – it is entirely dependent upon the degree of conviction. As doubts vanish and you can feel "I AM this", you begin to develop the fruit or the nature of the thing you are feeling yourself to be.

When a person buys a new hat or pair of shoes, he thinks everyone knows that they are new. He feels unnatural with his newly acquired apparel until it becomes a part of him. The same applies to the wearing of the new states of consciousness.

When you ask yourself the question, "How would I feel if my desire were at this moment realized?", the automatic reply, until it is properly conditioned by time and use, is actually disturbing. The period of adjustment to realize this potential of consciousness is comparable to the newness of the wearing apparel.

Not knowing that consciousness is ever outpicturing itself in conditions round about you, like Lot's wife, you continually look back upon your problem and again become hypnotized by its seeming naturalness [Genesis 19].

Heed the words of Jesus (salvation):

> *Leave all and follow Me.*
>
> —Matthew 4:19 [Matthew 8:22; Matthew 16:24; Matthew 19:21; Mark 1:17; Mark 8:34; Mark 10:21; Luke 9:23; Luke 18:22

> *Let the dead bury the dead.*
>
> —Matthew 8:22; Luke 9:60

Your problem might have you so hypnotized by its seeming reality and naturalness that you find it difficult to wear the new feeling or consciousness of your savior. You must assume this garment if you would have results.

The stone (consciousness) which the builders rejected (would not wear) is the chief cornerstone, and other foundations no man can lay.

CHAPTER 10

To Him That Hath

Take heed therefore how ye hear; for whosoever hath, to him shall be given; and whosoever hath not, from him shall be taken even that which he seemeth to have.

—Luke 8:18

The Bible, which is the greatest psychological book ever written, warns man to be aware of what he hears; then follows this warning with the statement, "To him that hath it shall be given and to him that hath not it shall be taken away".

Though many look upon this statement as one of the most cruel and unjust of the sayings attributed to Jesus, it still remains a just and merciful law based upon life's changeless principle of expression.

Man's ignorance of the working of the law does not excuse him nor save him from the results.

Law is impersonal and therefore no respecter of persons [Acts 10:34; Romans 2:11].

Man is warned to be selective in that which he hears and accepts as true. Everything that man accepts as true leaves an impression on his consciousness and must in time be defined as proof or disproof.

Perceptive hearing is the perfect medium through which man registers impressions. A man must discipline himself to hear only that which he wants to hear, regardless of rumors or the evidence of his senses to the contrary. As he conditions his perceptive hearing, he will react only to those impressions which he has decided upon. This law never fails.

Fully conditioned, man becomes incapable of hearing other than that which contributes to his desire.

God, as you have discovered, is that unconditioned awareness which gives to you all that you are aware of being. To be aware of being or having anything is to be or have that which you are aware of being. Upon this changeless principle all things rest. It is impossible for anything to be other than that which it is aware of being.

"To him that hath (that which he is aware of being) it shall be given". Good, bad or indifferent – it does not matter – man receives multiplied a hundredfold that which he is aware of being. In keeping with this changeless law —"To him that hath not, it shall be taken from him and added to the one that hath"— the rich get richer and the poor get poorer. You can only magnify that which you are conscious of being.

All things gravitate to that consciousness with which they are in tune. Likewise, all things disentangle themselves from that consciousness with which they are out of tune.

Divide the wealth of the world equally among all men and in a short time, this equal division will be as originally disproportioned. Wealth will find its way back into the pockets of those from whom it was taken.

Instead of joining the chorus of the have-nots, who insist on destroying those who have, recognize this changeless law of expression. Consciously define yourself as that which you desire. Once defined, your conscious claim established, continue in this confidence until the reward is received. As surely as the day follows the night, any attribute, consciously claimed, will manifest itself.

Thus, that which to the sleeping orthodox world is a cruel and unjust law becomes to the enlightened one of the most merciful and just statements of truth.

I am come not to destroy but to fulfill.

—Matthew 5:17

Nothing is actually destroyed. Any seeming destruction is a result of a change in consciousness. Consciousness ever fills full the state in which it dwells. The state from which consciousness is detached seems to those not familiar with this law to be destructive. However, this is only preparatory to a new state of consciousness.

Claim yourself to be that which you want filled full.

Nothing is destroyed. All is fulfilled.
To him that hath it shall be given.

CHAPTER 11

Christmas

Behold, a virgin shall be with child and shall bring forth a Son, and they shall call His name Emmanuel, which being interpreted is God with us.

—Matthew 1:23

One of the most controversial statements in the New Testament concerns the virgin conception and subsequent birth of Jesus, a conception in which man had no part. It is recorded that a Virgin conceived a Son without the aid of man, then secretly and without effort gave birth to her conception. This is the foundation upon which all Christendom rests.

The Christian world is asked to believe this story, for man must believe the unbelievable to fully express the greatness that he is.

Scientifically, man might be inclined to discard the whole Bible as untrue because his reason will not permit him to believe that the virgin birth is physiologically possible; but the Bible is a message of the soul and must be interpreted psychologically if man is to discover its true symbology.

Man must see this story as a psychological drama rather than a statement of physical fact. In so doing, he will discover the Bible to be based on a law which, if self-applied, will result in a manifested expression transcending his wildest dreams of accomplishment. To apply this law of self-expression, man must be schooled in the belief and disciplined to stand upon the platform that "all things are possible to God" [Matthew 19:26; Mark 9:23; 10:27; 14:36; Luke 18:27; Acts 8:37].

The outstanding dramatic dates of the New Testament, namely, the birth, death and resurrection of Jesus, were timed and dated to coincide with certain astronomical phenomena. The mystics who recorded this story noticed that at certain seasons of the year beneficial changes on earth coincided with astronomical changes above. In writing this psychological drama, they have personified the story of the soul as the biography of man.

Using these cosmic changes, they have marked the Birth and Resurrection of Jesus to convey that the same beneficial changes take place psychologically in the consciousness of man as he follows the law.

Even to those who fail to understand it, the story of Christmas is one of the most beautiful stories ever told. When unfolded in the light of its mystic symbology, it is revealed as the true birth of every manifestation in the world.

This virgin birth is recorded as having taken place on December 25th or, as certain secret societies celebrate it, on Christmas Eve, at midnight of December 24th.

Mystics established this date to mark the birth of Jesus because it was in keeping with the great earthly benefits this astronomical change signifies.

The astronomical observations which prompted the authors of this drama to use these dates were all made in the northern hemisphere; so from an astronomical point of view, the reverse would be true if seen from the southern latitudes.

However, this story was recorded in the north and therefore was based on northern observation.

Man very early discovered that the sun played a most important part in his life, that without the sun, physical life as he knew it could not be. So these most important dates in the story of the life of Jesus are based upon the position of the sun as seen from the earth in the northern latitudes.

After the sun reaches its highest point in the heavens in June, it gradually falls southward, taking with it the life of the plant world so that by December almost all of nature has been stilled. Should the sun continue to fall southward, all nature would be stilled unto death.

However, on December 25th, the sun begins its great move northward, bringing with it the promise of salvation and life anew for the world. Each day, as the sun rises higher in the heavens, man gains confidence in being saved from death by cold and starvation, for he knows that as it moves northward and crosses the equator all nature will rise again, will be resurrected from its long winter sleep.

Our day is measured from midnight to midnight, and, since the visible day begins in the east and ends in the west, the ancients said the day was born of that constellation which occupied the eastern horizon at midnight. On Christmas Eve, or midnight of December 24th, the constellation Virgo is rising on the eastern horizon.

So it is recorded that this Son and Savior of the world was born of a virgin.

It is also recorded that this virgin mother was traveling through the night, that she stopped at an inn and was given the only available room among the animals and there in a manger, where the animals fed, the shepherds found the Holy Child.

The animals with whom the Holy Virgin was lodged are the holy animals of the zodiac. There in that constantly moving circle of astronomical animals stands the Holy Mother, Virgo, and there you will see her every midnight of December 24th, standing on the eastern horizon as the sun and savior of the world starts his journey northward.

Psychologically, this birth takes place in man on that day when man discovers his consciousness to be the sun and savior of his world. When man knows the significance of this mystical statement, "I am the light of the world" [Matthew 5:14; John 8:12], he will realize that his I AM, or consciousness, is the sun of his life, which sun radiates images upon the screen of space. These images are in the likeness of that which he, as man, is conscious of being. Thus qualities and attributes which appear to move upon the screen of his world are really projections of this light from within himself.

The numberless unrealized hopes and ambitions of man are the seeds which are buried within the consciousness or virgin womb of man. There they remain like the seeds of earth, held in the frozen waste of winter, waiting for the sun to move northward or for man to return to the knowledge of who he is. In returning he moves northward through recognition of his true self by claiming "I AM the light of the world".

When man discovers his consciousness or I AM to be God, the savior of his world, he will be as the sun in its northern passage.

All hidden urges and ambitions will then be warmed and stimulated into birth by this knowledge of his true self. He will claim that he is that which heretofore he hoped to be. Without the aid of any man, he will define himself as that which he desires to express.

He will discover that his I AM is the virgin conceiving without the aid of man, that all conceptions of himself, when felt, and fixed in consciousness, will be embodied easily as living realities in his world.

Man will one day realize that this whole drama takes place in his consciousness, that his unconditioned consciousness or I AM is the Virgin Mary desiring to express, that through this law of self-expression he defines himself as that which he desires to express, and that without the help or cooperation of anyone he will express that which he has consciously claimed and defined himself as being.

He will then understand why Christmas is fixed on December 25th, while Easter is a movable date; why upon the virgin conception the whole of Christendom rests; that his consciousness is the virgin womb or bride of the Lord receiving impressions as self-impregnations and then, without assistance, embodying these impressions as the expressions of his life.

CHAPTER 12

Crucifixion & Resurrection

I AM the Resurrection and the Life; he that believeth in Me, though he were dead, yet shall he live.

—John 11:25

The mystery of the crucifixion and the resurrection is so interwoven that, to be fully understood, the two must be explained together for one determines the other. This mystery is symbolized on earth in the rituals of Good Friday and Easter. You have observed that the anniversary of this cosmic event, announced every year by the church, is not a fixed date as are other anniversaries marking births and deaths, but that this day changes from year to year, falling anywhere from the 22nd day of March to the 25th day of April.

The day of resurrection is determined in this manner. The first Sunday after the full moon in Aries is celebrated as Easter. Aries begins on the 21st day of March and ends approximately on the 19th day of April. The sun's entry into Aries marks the beginning of Spring. The moon in its monthly transit around the earth will form sometime between March 21st and April 25th an opposition to the sun, which opposition is called a full moon. The first Sunday after this phenomenon of the heavens occurs is celebrated as Easter; the Friday preceding this day is observed as Good Friday.

This movable date should tell the observant one to look for some interpretation other than the one commonly accepted. These days do not mark the anniversaries of the death and resurrection of an individual who lived on earth.

Seen from the earth, the sun in its northern passage appears at the Spring season of the year to cross the imaginary line man calls the equator. So it is said by the mystic to be crossified or crucified that man might live. It is significant that soon after this event takes place, all nature begins to arise or resurrect itself from its long Winter's sleep. Therefore, it may be concluded that this disturbance of nature, at this season of the year, is due directly to this crossing. Thus, it is believed that the sun must shed its blood on the Passover.

If these days marked the death and resurrection of a man, they would be fixed so that they would fall on the same date every year as all other historical events are fixed, but obviously this is not the case.

These dates were not intended to mark the anniversaries of the death and resurrection of Jesus, the man. The scriptures are psychological dramas and will reveal their meaning only as they are interpreted psychologically. These dates are adjusted to coincide with the cosmic change which occurs at this time of the year, marking the death of the old year and the beginning or resurrecting of the new year or Spring. These dates do symbolize the death and resurrection of the Lord; but this Lord is not a man; it is your awareness of being.

It is recorded that He gave His life that you might live, "I AM come that you might have life and that you might have it more abundantly" [John 10:10]. Consciousness slays itself by detaching itself from that which it is conscious of being so that it may live to that which it desires to be.

Spring is the time of year when the millions of seeds, which all Winter lay buried in the ground, suddenly spring into visibility that man might live; and, because the mystical drama of the crucifixion and resurrection is in the nature of this yearly change, it is celebrated at this Spring season of the year; but, actually, it is taking place every moment of time.

The being who is crucified is your awareness of being. The cross is your conception of yourself. The resurrection is the lifting into visibility of this conception of yourself.

Far from being a day of mourning, Good Friday should be a day of rejoicing, for there can be no resurrection or expression unless there is first a crucifixion or impression.

The thing to be resurrected in your case is that which you desire to be. To do this, you must feel yourself to be the thing desired. You must feel "I AM the resurrection and the life of the desire".

I AM (your awareness of being) is the power resurrecting and making alive that which in your awareness you desire to be.

"Two shall agree on touching anything and I shall establish it on earth"

> *Again I say unto you, That if two of you shall agree on earth as touching any thing that they shall ask, it shall be done for them of my Father which is in heaven.*
>
> —Matthew 18:19

The two agreeing are you (your awareness – the consciousness desiring) and the thing desired. When this agreement is attained, the crucifixion is completed; two have crossed or crossified each other.

I AM and THAT – consciousness and that which you are conscious of being – have joined and are one; I AM now nailed or fixed in the belief that I AM this fusion.

Jesus or I AM is nailed upon the cross of that. The nail that binds you upon the cross is the nail of feeling.

The mystical union is now consummated and the result will be the birth of a child or the resurrection of a son bearing witness of his Father.

Consciousness is united to that which it is conscious of being. The world of expression is the child confirming this union.

The day you cease to be conscious of being that which you are now conscious of being, that day your child or expression shall die and return to the bosom of his father, the faceless, formless awareness.

All expressions are the results of such mystical unions.

So the priests are correct when they say that true marriages are made in heaven and can only be dissolved in heaven.

But let me clarify this statement by telling you that heaven is not a locality; it is a state of consciousness.

The Kingdom of Heaven is within you.

—Luke 17:21

In heaven (consciousness) God is touched by that which he is aware of being. "Who has touched me? For I perceive virtue has gone out of me."

'Who touched me?' And Jesus said, 'Somebody hath touched me: for I perceive that virtue is gone out of me'.

—Luke 8:45,46; Mark 5:30

The moment this touching (feeling) takes place, there is an offspring or going-out-of-me into visibility taking place.

The day man feels "I AM free", "I AM wealthy", "I AM strong", God (I AM) is touched or crucified by these qualities or virtues.

The results of such touching or crucifying will be seen in the birth or resurrection of the qualities felt, for man must have visible confirmation of all that he is conscious of being.

Now you will know why man or manifestation is always made in the image of God. Your awareness imag[in]es and outpictures all that you are aware of being.

I AM the Lord and besides me there is no God.

—Isaiah 45:5,6

I AM the Resurrection and the Life.

—John 11:25

You shall become fixed in the belief that you are that which you desire to be. Before you have any visible proof that you are, you will, from the deep conviction which you have felt fixed within you, know that you are; and so, without waiting for the confirmation of your senses, you will cry, "It is finished" [John 19:30].

Then, with a faith born of the knowledge of this changeless law, you will be as one dead and entombed; you will be still and unmoved in your conviction and confident that you will resurrect the qualities that you have fixed and are feeling within you.

CHAPTER 13

The I'm-Pressions

And as we have borne the image of the earthly, we shall also bear the image of the heavenly.

—1 Cor. 15:49

Your consciousness or your I AM is the unlimited potential upon which impressions are made. I'm-pressions are defined states pressed upon your I AM. Your consciousness or your I AM can be likened to a sensitive film. In the virgin state, it is potentially unlimited.

You can impress or record a message of love or a hymn of hate, a wonderful symphony or discordant jazz. It does not matter what the nature of the impression might be; your I AM will, without a murmur, willingly receive and sustain all impressions.

Your consciousness is the one referred to in Isaiah 53:3-7:

He is despised and rejected of men; a man of sorrows, and acquainted with grief: and we hid as it were our faces from Him, He was despised, and we esteemed Him not.

Surely He hath borne our grieves, and carried our sorrows: yet we did esteem Him stricken, smitten of God, and afflicted.

But He was wounded for our transgressions, He was bruised for our iniquities: the chastisement of our peace was upon him; and with his stripes we are healed.

All we like sheep have gone astray; we have turned every one to his own way; and the Lord hath laid on Him the iniquity of us all.

He was oppressed, and He was afflicted,
yet He opened not his mouth:
He is brought as a lamb to the slaughter
and as a sheep before her shearers is dumb,
so He openeth not His mouth.

Your unconditioned consciousness is impersonal; it is no respecter of persons.

—Acts 10:34; Romans 2:11

Without thought or effort, it automatically expresses every impression that is registered upon it. It does not object to any impression that is placed upon it for; although it is capable of receiving and expressing any and all defined states, it remains forever an immaculate and an unlimited potential.

Your I AM is the foundation upon which the defined state or conception of yourself rests; but it is not defined by, nor is it dependent on, such defined states for its being.

Your I AM neither expands nor contracts; nothing alters or adds to it. Before any defined state was, IT is. When all states cease to be, IT is. All defined states or conceptions of yourself are but ephemeral expressions of your eternal being.

To be impressed is to be I'm-pressed (I AM pressed – first person – present tense). All expressions are the result of I'm-pressions. Only as you claim yourself to be that which you desire to be will you express such desires.

Let all desires become impressions of qualities that are, not of qualities that will be. I'm (your awareness) is God, and God is the fullness of all, the Eternal NOW, I AM.

Take no thought of tomorrow; tomorrow's expressions are determined by today's impressions.

Now is the accepted time.

—2 Cor. 6:2, Isa. 49:8

The Kingdom of Heaven is at hand.

—Matthew 4:17

Jesus (salvation) said:

I am with you always.

—Matthew 28:20

Your awareness is the savior that is with you always; but, if you deny Him, He will deny you also [Matthew 10:33; Luke 12:9]. You deny Him by claiming that He will appear, as millions today are claiming that salvation is to come; this is the equivalent of saying, "We are not saved".

You must stop looking for your savior to appear and begin claiming that you are already saved, and the signs of your claims will follow.

When the widow was asked what she had in her house, there was recognition of substance; her claim was a few drops of oil [Kings 4:1-6]. A few drops will become a gusher if properly claimed. Your awareness magnifies all consciousness.

To claim that I shall have oil (joy) is to confess that I have empty measures. Such impressions of lack produce lack.

God, your awareness, is no respecter of persons [Acts 10:34; Romans 2:11]. Purely impersonal, God, this awareness of all existence, receives impressions, qualities and attributes defining consciousness — namely, your impressions.

Your every desire should be determined by need. Needs, whether seeming or real, will automatically be fulfilled when they are welcomed with sufficient intensity of purpose as defined desires.

Knowing that your awareness is God, you should look upon each desire as the spoken word of God, telling you that which is.

Cease ye from man, whose breath is in his nostrils: for wherein is he to be accounted of?

—Isaiah 2:22

We are ever that which is defined by our awareness. Never claim, "I shall be that". Let all claims from now on be, "I AM that I AM". Before we ask, we are answered. The solution of any problem associated with desire is obvious. Every problem automatically produces the desire of solution.

Man is schooled in the belief that his desires are things against which he must struggle. In his ignorance, he denies his savior who is constantly knocking at the door of consciousness to be let in (I AM the door).

Would not your desire, if realized, save you from your problem?

To let your savior in is the easiest thing in the world. Things must be, to be let in.

You are conscious of a desire; the desire is something you are aware of now. Your desire, though invisible, must be affirmed by you to be something that is real.

> *God calleth those things which be not (are not seen) as though they were.*
>
> —Romans 4:17

Claiming I AM the thing desired, I let the savior in.

> *Behold, I stand at the door, and knock: if any man hear My voice, and open the door, I will come in to him, and will sup with him, and he with Me.*
>
> —Revelation 3:20

Every desire is the savior's knock at the door.

This knock every man hears.

Man opens the door when he claims, "I AM He". See to it that you let your savior in.

Let the thing desired press itself upon you until you are I'm-pressed with nowness of your savior; then you utter the cry of victory:

> *It is finished.*
>
> —John 19:30

CHAPTER 14

Circumcision

In whom also ye are circumcised with the circumcision made without hands; in putting off the body of the sins of the flesh by circumcision of Christ.

—Col. 2:11

Circumcision is the operation which removes the veil that hides the head of creation. The physical act has nothing to do with the spiritual act.

The whole world could be physically circumcised and yet remain unclean and blind leaders of the blind.

The spiritually circumcised have had the veil of darkness removed and know themselves to be Christ, the light of the world.

Let me now perform the spiritual operation on you, the reader.

This act is performed on the eighth day after birth, not because this day has any special significance or in any way differs from other days, but it is performed on this eighth day because eight is the figure which has neither beginning nor end.

Furthermore, the ancients symbolized the eighth numeral or letter as an enclosure or veil within and behind which lay buried the mystery of creation.

Thus, the secret of the operation on the eighth day is in keeping with the nature of the act, which act is to reveal the eternal head of creation, that changeless something in which all things begin and end and yet which remains its eternal self when all things cease to be.

This mysterious something is your awareness of being. At this moment you are aware of being, but you are also aware of being someone. This someone is the veil that hides the being you really are.

You are first conscious of being, then you are conscious of being man. After the veil of man is placed upon your faceless self, you become conscious of being a member of a certain race, nation, family, creed etc.

The veil to be lifted in spiritual circumcision is the veil of man. But before this can be done, you must cut away the adhesions of race, nation, family and so on.

> *In Christ there is neither Greek nor Jew, bond nor free, male nor female.*
>
> *...a renewal in which there is no distinction between Greek and Jew, circumcised and uncircumcised, barbarian, Scythian, slave and freeman, but Christ is all, and in all.*
>
> —Colossians 3:11

> *You must leave father, mother, brother and follow me.*
>
> *If anyone comes to Me, and does not hate his own father and mother and wife and children and brothers and sisters, yes, and even his own life, he cannot be My disciple.*
>
> —Luke 14:26

To accomplish this you stop identifying yourself with these divisions by becoming indifferent to such claims. Indifference is the knife that severs. Feeling is the tie that binds.

When you can look upon man as one grand brotherhood without distinction of race or creed, then you will know that you have severed these adhesions.

With these ties cut, all that now separates you from your true being is your belief that you are man.

To remove this last veil, you drop your conception of yourself as man by knowing yourself just to be.

Instead of the consciousness of "I AM man", let there be just "I AM" – faceless, formless, and without figure.

You are spiritually circumcised when the consciousness of man is dropped and your unconditioned awareness of being is revealed to you as the everlasting head of creation, a formless, faceless all-knowing presence.

Then, unveiled and awake, you will declare and know that – I AM is God and beside me, this awareness, there is no God.

This mystery is told symbolically in the Bible story of Jesus washing the feet of his disciples. It is recorded that Jesus laid aside his garments and took a towel and girded himself. Then, after washing his disciples' feet, he wiped them with the towel wherewith he was girded. Peter protested the washing of his feet and was told that unless his feet were washed he would have no part of Jesus. Peter on hearing this replied, "Lord, not my feet only, but also my hands and my head". Jesus answered and said, "He that is washed needeth not save to wash his feet, but is clean every whit" [John 13:1-10].

Common sense would tell the reader that a man is not clean all over just, because his feet are washed. Therefore, he should either discard this story as fantastic or else look for its hidden meaning.

Every story of the Bible is a psychological drama taking place in the consciousness of man, and this one is no exception. This washing of the disciples' feet is the mystical story of spiritual circumcision or the revealing of the secrets of the Lord.

Jesus is called the Lord. You are told that the Lord's name is I AM – Je Suis. "I AM the Lord that is my name" [Isaiah 42:8]. The story states that Jesus was naked save for a towel which covered his loins or secrets. Jesus or Lord symbolizes your awareness of being whose secrets are hidden by the towel (consciousness of man). The foot symbolizes the understanding which must be washed of all human beliefs or conceptions of itself by the Lord. As the towel is removed to dry the feet, the secrets of the Lord are revealed.

In short, the removing of the belief that you are man reveals your awareness as the head of creation. Man is the foreskin hiding the head of creation. I AM the Lord hidden by the veil of man.

CHAPTER 15

Interval of Time

Let not your heart be troubled; ye believe in God, believe also in me. In my Father's house are many mansions; if it were not so, I would have told you. I go to prepare a place for you. And if I go and prepare a place for you, I will come again, and receive you unto myself; that where I am, there ye may be also.

—John 14:1-3

The ME in whom you must believe is your consciousness, the I AM; it is God. It is also the Father's house containing within itself all conceivable states of consciousness. Every conditioned state of consciousness is called a mansion.

This conversation takes place within yourself. Your I AM, the unconditioned consciousness, is the Christ Jesus speaking to the conditioned self or the John Smith consciousness.

"I AM John", from a mystical point of view, is two beings, namely, Christ and John.

So I go to prepare a place for you, moving from your present state of consciousness into that state desired. It is a promise by your Christ or awareness of being to your present conception of yourself that you will leave your present consciousness and appropriate another.

Man is such a slave to time that, if after he has appropriated a state of consciousness which is not now seen by the world and it, the appropriated state, does not immediately embody itself, he loses faith in his unseen claim; forthwith he drops it and returns to his former static state of being.

Because of this limitation of man, I have found it very helpful to employ a specified interval of time in making this journey into a prepared mansion.

Wait but a little while.

—Job 36:2

We have all catalogued the different days of the week, months of the year and seasons. By this, I mean you and I have said time and again, "Why, today feels just like Sunday" or "Monday" or "Saturday". We have also said in the middle of Summer, "Why, this feels and looks like the Fall of the year".

This is positive proof that you and I have definite feelings associated with these different days, months, and seasons of the year. Because of this association, we can at any time consciously dwell in that day or season which we have selected.

Do not selfishly define this interval in days and hours because you are anxious to receive it, but simply remain in the conviction that it is done – time, being purely relative, should be eliminated entirely – and your desire will be fulfilled.

This ability to dwell at any point in time permits us to employ time in our travel into the desired mansion.

Now I (consciousness) go to a point in time and there prepare a place. If I go to such a point in time and prepare a place, I shall return to this point in time where I have left; and I shall pick up and take you with me into that place which I have prepared, that where I AM, there ye may also be.

Let me give you an example of this travel.

Suppose you had an intense desire. Like most men who are enslaved by time, you might feel that you could not possibly realize so large a desire in a limited interval. But admitting that all things are possible to God, believing God to be the ME within you or your consciousness of being, you can say,

"As John, I can do nothing; but since all things are possible to God and God I know to be my consciousness of being, I can realize my desire in a little while. How my desire will be realized I do not (as John) know, but by the very law of my being I do know that it shall be."

With this belief firmly established, decide what would be a relative, rational interval of time in which such a desire could be realized.

Again, let me remind you not to shorten the interval of time because you are anxious to receive your desire; make it a natural interval. No one can give you the time interval. Only you can say what the natural interval would be to you. The interval of time is relative; that is, no two individuals would give the same measurement of time for the realization of their desire.

Time is ever conditioned by man's conception of himself. Confidence in yourself as determined by conditioned consciousness always shortens the interval of time.

If you were accustomed to great accomplishments, you would give yourself a much shorter interval in which to accomplish your desire than the man schooled in defeat.

If today were Wednesday and you decided that it would be quite possible for your desire to embody a new realization of yourself by Sunday, then Sunday becomes the point in time that you would visit.

To make this visit, you shut out Wednesday and let in Sunday. This is accomplished by simply feeling that it is Sunday. Begin to hear the church bells; begin to feel the quietness of the day and all that Sunday means to you; actually feel that it is Sunday.

When this is accomplished, feel the joy of having received that which on Wednesday was but a desire. Feel the complete thrill of having received it, and then return to Wednesday, the point in time you left behind you.

In doing this, you created a vacuum in consciousness by moving from Wednesday to Sunday. Nature, abhorring vacuums, rushes in to fill it, thereby fashioning a mould in the likeness of that which you potentially create, namely, the joy of having realized your defined desire.

As you return to Wednesday, you will be filled with a joyful expectancy, because you have established the consciousness of that which must take place the following Sunday.

As you walk through the interval of Thursday, Friday, and Saturday, nothing disturbs you regardless of conditions, because you predetermined that which you would be on the Sabbath and that remains an unalterable conviction.

Having gone before and prepared the place, you have returned to John and are now taking him with you through the interval of three days into the prepared place that he might share your joy with you, for where I AM, "there ye may also be".

CHAPTER 16

The Triune God

And God said, Let Us make man in Our image, after Our likeness.

—Gen. 1:26

Having discovered God to be our awareness of being and this unconditioned changeless reality (the I AM) to be the only creator, let us see why the Bible records a trinity as the creator of the world.

In the 26th verse of the first chapter of Genesis, it is stated:

And God said, Let Us make man in Our image.

The churches refer to this plurality of Gods as God the Father, God the Son, and God the Holy Spirit.

What is meant by "God the Father, God the Son, and God the Holy Spirit", they have never attempted to explain, for they are in the dark concerning this mystery.

The Father, Son, and Holy Spirit are three aspects or conditions of the unconditioned awareness of being called God.

The consciousness of being precedes the consciousness of being something. That unconditioned awareness which preceded all states of awareness is God – I AM.

The three conditioned aspects or divisions of itself can best be told in this manner:

The *receptive attitude of mind* is that aspect which receives impressions and therefore may be likened to a womb or Mother.

That which makes the impression is the male or pressing aspect and is therefore known as Father.

The impression in time becomes an *expression*, which expression is ever the likeness and image of the impression; therefore this objectified aspect is said to be the Son bearing witness of his Father-Mother.

An understanding of this mystery of the trinity enables the one who understands it to completely transform his world and fashion it to his own liking.

Here is a practical application of this mystery.

Sit quietly and decide what it is you would like most to express or possess. After you have decided, close your eyes and take your attention completely away from all that would deny the realization of the thing desired; then assume a receptive attitude of mind and play the game of supposing by imagining how you would feel if you were now to realize your desire.

Begin to listen as though space were talking to you and telling you that you are now that which you desire to be.

This receptive attitude is the state of consciousness that you must assume before an impression can be made.

As this pliable and impressive state of mind is attained, then begin to impress upon yourself the fact that you are that which you desired to be by claiming and feeling that you are now expressing and possessing that which you had decided to be and to have.

Continue in this attitude until the impression is made.

As you contemplate being and possessing that which you have decided to be and to have, you will notice that with every inhalation of breath a joyful thrill courses through your entire being.

This thrill increases in intensity as you feel more and more the joy of being that which you are claiming yourself to be.

Then in one final deep inhalation, your whole being will explode with the joy of accomplishment, and you will know by your feeling that you are impregnated by God, the Father.

As soon as the impression is made, open your eyes and return to the world that but a few moments before you had shut out.

In this receptive attitude of yours, while you contemplated being that which you desired to be, you were actually performing the spiritual act of generation; so you are now on your return from this silent meditation a pregnant being bearing a child or impression, which child was immaculately conceived without the aid of man.

Doubt is the only force capable of disturbing the seed or impression; to avoid a miscarriage of so wonderful a child, walk in secrecy through the necessary interval of time that it will take the impression to become an expression.

Tell no man of your spiritual romance. Lock your secret within you in joy, confident and happy that some day you will bear the son of your lover by expressing and possessing the nature of your impression.

Then will you know the mystery of "God said, 'Let Us make man in Our image'".

You will know that the plurality of Gods referred to is the three aspects of your own consciousness and that you are the trinity, meeting in a spiritual conclave to fashion a world in the image and likeness of that which you are conscious of being.

CHAPTER 17

Prayer

When thou prayest, enter into thy closet, and when thou hast shut thy door, pray to thy Father which is in secret; and thy Father which seeth in secret shall reward thee openly.

—Matt. 6:6

What things soever ye desire, when ye pray, believe that ye receive them, and ye shall have them.

—Mark 11:24

Prayer is the most wonderful experience man can have.

Unlike the daily murmurings of the vast majority of mankind in all lands who by their vain repetitions hope to gain the ear of God, prayer is the ecstasy of a spiritual wedding taking place in the deep, silent stillness of consciousness.

In its true sense prayer is God's marriage ceremony. Just as a maid on her wedding day relinquishes the name of her family to assume the name of her husband, in like manner, one who prays must relinquish his present name or nature and assume the nature of that for which he prays.

The gospels have clearly instructed man as to the performance of this ceremony in the following manner:

When ye pray go within in secret and shut the door and your Father who sees in secret will reward you openly.

—Matthew 6:6

The going within is the entering of the bridal chamber. Just as no one but the bride and groom are permitted to enter so holy a room as the bridal suite on the night of the marriage ceremony, likewise no one but the one who prays and that for which he prays are permitted to enter the holy hour of prayer. As the bride and groom on entering the bridal suite securely shut the door against the outside world, so too must the one who enters the holy hour of prayer close the door of the senses and entirely shut out the world round about him.

This is accomplished by taking the attention completely away from all things other than that with which you are now in love (the thing desired).

The second phase of this spiritual ceremony is defined in these words:

When ye pray, believe that ye receive, and ye shall receive.

As you joyfully contemplate being and possessing that which you desire to be and to have, you have taken this second step and are therefore spiritually performing the acts of marriage and generation.

Your receptive attitude of mind while praying or contemplating can be likened to a bride or womb for it is that aspect of mind which receives the impressions.

That which you contemplate being is the groom, for it is the name or nature you assume and therefore is that which leaves its impregnation; so one dies to maidenhood or present nature as one assumes the name and nature of the impregnation.

Lost in contemplation and having assumed the name and nature of the thing contemplated, your whole being thrills with the joy of being it. This thrill, which runs through your entire being as you appropriate the consciousness of your desire, is the proof that you are both married and impregnated.

As you return from this silent meditation, the door is once more opened upon the world you had left behind. But this time you return as a pregnant bride.

You enter the world a changed being and, although no one but you knows of this wonderful romance, the world will, in a very short while, see the signs of your pregnancy, for you will begin to express that which you in your hour of silence felt yourself to be.

The mother of the world or bride of the Lord is purposely called Mary, or water, for water loses its identity as it assumes the nature of that with which it is mixed. Likewise, Mary, the receptive attitude of mind, must lose its identity as it assumes the nature of the thing desired.

Only as one is willing to give up his present limitations and identity can he become that which he desires to be.

Prayer is the formula by which such divorces and marriages are accomplished.

> *Two shall agree as touching anything and it shall be established on earth.*
>
> —Matthew 18:19

The two agreeing are you, the bride, and the thing desired, the groom.

As this agreement is accomplished, a son bearing witness of this union will be born. You begin to express and possess that which you are conscious of being.

Praying, then, is recognizing yourself to be that which you desire to be rather than begging God for that which you desire.

Millions of prayers are daily unanswered because man prays to a God who does not exist.

Consciousness being God, one must seek in consciousness for the thing desired by assuming the consciousness of the quality desired. Only as one does this will his prayers be answered.

To be conscious of being poor while praying for riches is to be rewarded with that which you are conscious of being, namely, poverty.

Prayers, to be successful, must be claimed and appropriated. Assume the positive consciousness of the thing desired.

With your desire defined, quietly go within and shut the door behind you. Lose yourself in your desire; feel yourself to be one with it; remain in this fixation until you have absorbed the life and name by claiming and feeling yourself to be and to have that which you desired.

When you emerge from the hour of prayer, you must do so conscious of being and possessing that which you heretofore desired.

CHAPTER 18

The Twelve Disciples

And when He had called unto Him His twelve disciples, He gave them power against unclean spirits, to cast them out, and to heal all manner of sickness and all manner of disease.

—Matt. 10:1

The twelve disciples represent the twelve qualities of mind which can be controlled and disciplined by man. If disciplined, they will at all times obey the command of the one who has disciplined them.

These twelve qualities in man are potentials of every mind. Undisciplined, their actions resemble more the actions of a mob than they do of a trained and disciplined army. All the storms and confusions that engulf man can be traced directly to these twelve ill-related characteristics of the human mind in its present slumbering state.

Until they are awakened and disciplined, they will permit every rumor and sensuous emotion to move them.

When these twelve are disciplined and brought under control, the one who accomplishes this control will say to them, "Hereafter I call you not slaves, but friends."

Henceforth I call you not servants for the servant knoweth not what his lord doeth but I have called you friends, for all things that I have heard of My Father I have made known unto you.

—John 15:15

He knows that from that moment on, each acquired disciplined attribute of mind will befriend and protect him.

The names of the twelve qualities reveal their natures. These names are not given to them until they are called to discipleship.

They are: Simon, who was later surnamed Peter, Andrew, James, John, Philip, Bartholomew, Thomas, Matthew, James the son of Alphaeus, Thaddaeus, Simon the Canaanite, and Judas [Matthew 10; Mark 1; Mark 3; Luke 6].

The first quality to be called and disciplined is Simon, or the attribute of hearing.

This faculty, when lifted to the level of a disciple, permits only such impressions to reach consciousness as those which his hearing has commanded him to let enter. No matter what the wisdom of man might suggest or the evidence of his senses convey, if such suggestions and ideas are not in keeping with that which he hears, he remains unmoved. This one has been instructed by his Lord and made to understand that every suggestion he permits to pass his gate will, on reaching his Lord and Master (his consciousness), leave its impression there, which impression must in time become an expression.

The instruction to Simon is that he should permit only dignified and honorable visitors or impressions to enter the house (consciousness) of his Lord. No mistake can be covered up or hidden from his Master, for every expression of life tells his Lord whom he consciously or unconsciously entertained.

When Simon, by his works, proves himself to be a true and faithful disciple, then he receives the surname of Peter, or the rock, the unmoved disciple, the one who cannot be bribed or coerced by any visitor. He is called by his Lord Simon Peter, the one who faithfully hears the commands of his Lord and besides which commands he hears not.

It is this Simon Peter who discovers the I AM to be Christ, and for his discovery is given the keys to heaven, and is made the foundation stone upon which the Temple of God rests.

Buildings must have firm foundations and only the disciplined hearing can, on learning that the I AM is Christ, remain firm and unmoved in the knowledge that I AM Christ and beside ME there is no savior.

The second quality to be called to discipleship is Andrew, or courage.

As the first quality, faith in oneself, is developed, it automatically calls into being its brother, courage.

Faith in oneself, which asks no man's help but quietly and alone appropriates the consciousness of the quality desired and – in spite of reason or the evidence of his senses to the contrary continues faithful-patiently waiting in the knowledge that his unseen claim if sustained must be realized – such faith develops a courage and strength of character that are beyond the wildest dreams of the undisciplined man whose faith is in things seen.

The faith of the undisciplined man cannot really be called faith. For if the armies, medicines or wisdom of man in which his faith is placed be taken from him, his faith and courage go with it. But from the disciplined one the whole world could be taken and yet he would remain faithful in the knowledge that the state of consciousness in which he abides must in due season embody itself. This courage is Peter's brother Andrew, the disciple, who knows what it is to dare, to do and to be silent.

The next two (third & fourth) who are called are also related. These are the brothers, James and John. James the just, the righteous judge, and his brother John, the beloved.

Justice to be wise must be administered with love, ever turning the other cheek and at all times returning good for evil, love for hate, non-violence for violence.

The disciple James, symbol of a disciplined judgment, must, when raised to the high office of a supreme judge, be blindfolded that he may not be influenced by the flesh nor judge after the appearances of being. Disciplined judgment is administered by one who is not influenced by appearances.

The one who has called these brothers to discipleship continues faithful to his command to hear only that which he has been commanded to hear, namely, the Good.

The man who has this quality of his mind disciplined is incapable of hearing and accepting as true anything – either of himself or another – which does not on the hearing fill his heart with love.

These two disciples or aspects of the mind are one and inseparable when awakened.

Such a disciplined one forgives all men for being that which they are. He knows as a wise judge that every man perfectly expresses that which he is, as man, conscious of being.

He knows that upon the changeless foundation of consciousness all manifestation rests, that changes of expression can be brought about only through changes of consciousness.

With neither condemnation nor criticism, these disciplined qualities of the mind permit everyone to be that which he is. However, although allowing this perfect freedom of choice to all, they are nevertheless ever watchful to see that they themselves prophesy and do – both for others and themselves – only such things which when expressed glorify, dignify and give joy to the expresser.

The fifth quality called to discipleship is Philip.

This one asked to be shown the Father. The awakened man knows that the Father is the state of consciousness in which man dwells, and that this state or Father can be seen only as it is expressed.

He knows himself to be the perfect likeness or image of that consciousness with which he is identified.

So he declares, "No man has at any time seen My Father; but I, the Son, who dwelleth in His bosom have revealed Him."

> *No one has seen God at any time; the only begotten God who is in the bosom of the Father, He has explained Him; therefore, when you see Me, the Son, you see My Father, for I come to bear witness of My Father.*
>
> —John 1:18

> *If ye had known Me, ye should have known My Father also: and from henceforth ye know Him, and have seen Him.*
>
> —John 14-7

> *Have I been so long time with you, and yet hast thou not known Me, Philip? He that hath seen Me hath seen the Father; and how sayest thou then, Shew us the Father? Believest thou not that I am in the Father, and the Father in Me? The words that I speak unto you I speak not of Myself; but the Father that dwelleth in Me, He doeth the works. Believe Me that I am in the Father, and the Father in Me; or else believe Me for the very works' sake.*
>
> —John 14:9-11

I and My Father, consciousness and its expression, God and man, are one.

This aspect of the mind, when disciplined, persists until ideas, ambitions and desires become embodied realities. This is the quality which states "Yet in my flesh shall I see God" [Job 19:26].

It knows how to make the word flesh [John 1:14], how to give form to the formless.

The sixth disciple is called Bartholomew.

This quality is the imaginative faculty, which quality of the mind when once awake distinguishes one from the masses.

An awakened imagination places the one so awakened head and shoulders above the average man, giving him the appearance of a beacon light in a world of darkness. No quality so separates man from man as does the disciplined imagination.

This is the separation of the wheat from the chaff. Those who have given most to Society are our artists, scientists, inventors, and others with vivid imaginations.

Should a survey be made to determine the reason why so many seemingly educated men and women fail in their after-college years, or should it be made to determine the reason for the different earning powers of the masses, there would be no doubt but that imagination played the important part.

Such a survey would show that it is imagination which makes one a leader while the lack of it makes one a follower.

Instead of developing the imagination of man, our educational system oftentimes stifles it by attempting to put into the mind of man the wisdom he seeks. It forces him to memorize a number of text books which, all too soon, are disproved by later text books.

Education is not accomplished by putting something into man; its purpose is to draw out of man the wisdom which is latent within him. May the reader call Bartholomew to discipleship, for only as this quality is raised to discipleship will you have the capacity to conceive ideas that will lift you beyond the limitations of man.

The seventh is called Thomas.

This disciplined quality doubts or denies every rumor and suggestion that are not in harmony with that which Simon Peter has been commanded to let enter.

The man who is conscious of being healthy (not because of inherited health, diets or climate, but because he is awakened and knows the state of consciousness in which he lives) will, in spite of the conditions of the world, continue to express health.

He could hear, through the press, radio and wise men of the world that a plague was sweeping the earth and yet he would remain unmoved and unimpressed. Thomas, the doubter – when disciplined – would deny that sickness or anything else which was not in sympathy with the consciousness to which he belonged had any power to affect him.

This quality of denial – when disciplined – protects man from receiving impressions that are not in harmony with his nature. He adopts an attitude of total indifference to all suggestions that are foreign to that which he desires to express. Disciplined denial is not a fight or a struggle but total indifference.

Matthew, the eighth, is the gift of God.

This quality of the mind reveals man's desires as gifts of God.

The man who has called this disciple into being knows that every desire of his heart is a gift from heaven and that it contains both the power and the plan of its self-expression.

Such a man never questions the manner of its expression. He knows that the plan of expression is never revealed to man for God's ways are past finding out [Romans 11:33].

He fully accepts his desires as gifts already received and goes his way in peace confident that they shall appear.

The ninth disciple is called James, the son of Alphaeus.

This is the quality of discernment. A clear and ordered mind is the voice which calls this disciple into being.

This faculty perceives that which is not revealed to the eye of man. This disciple judges not from appearances for it has the capacity to function in the realm of causes and so is never misled by appearances.

Clairvoyance is the faculty which is awakened when this quality is developed and disciplined; not the clairvoyance of the mediumistic séance rooms, but the true clairvoyance or clear seeing of the mystic. That is, this aspect of the mind has the capacity to interpret that which is seen. Discernment or the capacity to diagnose is the quality of James the son of Alphaeus.

Thaddaeus, the tenth, is the disciple of praise, a quality in which the undisciplined man is woefully lacking.

When this quality of praise and thanksgiving is awake within man, he walks with the words "Thank you, Father" ever on his lips.

He knows that his thanks for things not seen opens the windows of heaven and permits gifts beyond his capacity to receive to be poured upon him.

The man who is not thankful for things received is not likely to be the recipient of many gifts from the same source.

Until this quality of the mind is disciplined, man will not see the desert blossom as the rose. Praise and thanksgiving are to the invisible gifts of God (one's desires) what rain and sun are to the unseen seeds in the bosom of the earth.

The eleventh quality called is Simon of Canaan.

A good key phrase for this disciple is "hearing good news". Simon of Canaan, or Simon from the land of milk and honey, when called to discipleship, is proof that the one who calls this faculty into being has become conscious of the abundant life. He can say with the Psalmist David, "Thou preparest a table before me in the presence of mine enemies; thou anointest my head with oil; my cup runneth over" [Psalm 23:5]. This disciplined aspect of the mind is incapable of hearing anything other than good news and so is well qualified to preach the Gospel or Good-spell.

The twelfth and last of the disciplined qualities of the mind is called Judas.

When this quality is awake, man knows that he must die to that which he is before he can become that which he desires to be.

So it is said of this disciple that he committed suicide, which is the mystic's way of telling the initiated that Judas is the disciplined aspect of detachment.

This one knows that his I AM or consciousness is his savior, so he lets all other saviors go.

This quality – when disciplined – gives one the strength to let go.

The man who has called Judas into being has learned how to take his attention away from problems or limitations and to place it upon that which is the solution or savior.

> *Except ye be born again, you cannot in anywise enter the Kingdom of Heaven.*
>
> *Truly, truly, I say to you, unless one is born again, he cannot see the kingdom of God.*
>
> —John 3:3

> *No greater love hath man than this, that he give his life for a friend.*
>
> *Greater love hath no man than this, that a man lay down his life for his friends.*
>
> —John 15:13

When man realizes that the quality desired, if realized, would save and befriend him, he willingly gives up his life (present conception of himself) for his friend by detaching his consciousness from that which he is conscious of being and assuming the consciousness of that which he desires to be.

Judas, the one whom the world in its ignorance has blackened, will, when man awakes from his undisciplined state, be placed on high; for God is love and no greater love has a man than this – that he lay down his life for a friend.

Until man lets go of that which he is now conscious of being, he will not become that which he desires to be; and Judas is the one who accomplishes this through suicide or detachment.

These are the twelve qualities which were given to man in the foundation of the world.

Man's duty is to raise them to the level of discipleship. When this is accomplished, man will say:

> *I have finished the work which thou gavest Me to do. I have glorified Thee on earth and now, o, Father, glorify Thou Me with Thine own Self with the glory which I had with Thee before the world was.*
>
> —John 17:4, 5

CHAPTER 19

Liquid Light

In Him we live and move, and have our being.

—Acts 17:28

Psychically, this world appears as an ocean of light containing within itself all things, including man, as pulsating bodies enveloped in liquid light.

The Biblical story of the Flood [Genesis 6-8] is the state in which man lives.

Man is actually inundated in an ocean of liquid light in which countless numbers of light-beings move.

The story of the Flood is really being enacted today.

Man is the Ark containing within himself the male-female principles of every living thing.

The dove or idea which is sent out to find dry land is man's attempt to embody his ideas. Man's ideas resemble birds in flight – like the dove in the story, returning to man without finding a place to rest.

If man will not let such fruitless searches discourage him, one day the bird will return with a green sprig. After assuming the consciousness of the thing desired, he will be convinced that it is so; and he will feel and know that he is that which he has consciously appropriated, even though it is not yet confirmed by his senses.

One day man will become so identified with his conception that he will know it to be himself, and he will declare, "I AM; I AM that which

I desire to be (I AM that I AM)". He will find that, as he does so, he will begin to embody his desire (the dove or desire will this time find dry land), thereby realizing the mystery of the word made flesh.

Everything in the world is a crystallization of this liquid light. "I AM the light of the world" [John 8:12, John 9:5, John 12:46].

Your awareness of being is the liquid light of the world, which crystallizes into the conceptions you have of yourself.

Your unconditioned awareness of being first conceived itself in liquid light (which is the initial velocity of the universe). All things, from the highest to the lowest vibrations or expressions of life, are nothing more than the different vibrations of velocities of this initial velocity; gold, silver, iron, wood, flesh etc., are only different expressions or velocities of this one substance-liquid light.

All things are crystallized liquid light; the differentiation or infinity of expression is caused by the conceiver's desire to know himself.

Your conception of yourself automatically determines the velocity necessary to express that which you have conceived yourself to be.

The world is an ocean of liquid light in countless different states of crystallization.

CHAPTER 20

The Breath of Life

Then the LORD God formed man of dust from the ground, and breathed into his nostrils the breath of life; and man became a living being.

—Genesis 2:7

As thou knowest not what is the way of the spirit, nor how the bones do grow in the womb of her that is with child, even so thou knowest not the works of God who maketh all.

Just as you don't know how the breath of life enters the limbs of a child within its mother's womb, you also don't understand how God, who made everything, works.

—Ecclesiastes 11:5

And it came to pass after these things that the son of the woman, the mistress of the house, fell sick; and his sickness was so sore, that there was no breath left in him.

—1 Kings 17:17

And he (Elisha) went up and lay upon the child, and put his mouth upon his mouth, and his eyes upon his eyes, and his hands upon his hands, and stretched himself upon the child; and the flesh of the child waxed warm.

—2 Kings 4:34

> *But after the three and a half days, the breath of life from God came into them, and they stood on their feet; and great fear fell upon those who were watching them.*
>
> —Revelation 11:11

Did the Prophet Elijah [and/or Elisha] really restore to life the dead child of the Widow?

This story, along with all the other stories of the Bible, is a psychological drama which takes place in the consciousness of man.

The Widow symbolizes every man and woman in the world; the dead child represents the frustrated desires and ambitions of man; while the prophet, Elijah [and/or Elisha], symbolizes the God power within man, or man's awareness of being.

The story tells us that the prophet took the dead child from the Widow's bosom and carried him into an upper room. As he entered this upper room he closed the door behind them. Placing the child upon a bed, he breathed life into him. Returning to the mother, he gave her the child and said,

> *Woman, thy son liveth.*
>
> *See, thy son liveth.*
>
> —1 Kings 17:23, 2 Kings 4:36

Man's desires can be symbolized as the dead child. The mere fact that he desires is positive proof that the thing desired is not yet a living reality in his world. He tries in every conceivable way to nurse this desire into reality, to make it live, but finds in the end that all attempts are fruitless.

Most men are not aware of the existence of the infinite power within themselves as the prophet. They remain indefinitely with a dead child in their arms, not realizing that the desire is the positive indication of limitless capacities for its fulfillment.

Let man once recognize that his consciousness is a prophet who breathes life into all that he is conscious of being, and he will close the door of his senses against his problem and fix his attention – solely on that which he desires, knowing that by so doing, his desires are certain to be realized.

He will discover recognition to be the breath of life, for he will perceive – as he consciously claims himself to be now expressing or possessing all he desires to be or to have – that he will be breathing the breath [sic!] of life into his desire.

The quality claimed for the desire (in a way unknown to him) will begin to move and become a living reality in his world.

Yes, the Prophet Elijah [and/or Elisha] lives forever as man's limitless consciousness of being, the widow as his limited consciousness of being and the child as that which he desires to be.

CHAPTER 21

Daniel in the Lions' Den

Thy God whom thou servest continually; He will deliver thee.

—Daniel 6:16

The story of Daniel is the story of every man. It is recorded that Daniel, while locked in the lions' den, turned his back upon the hungry beasts; and with his vision turned toward the light coming from above, he prayed to the one and only God. The lions, who were purposely starved for the feast, remained powerless to hurt the prophet. Daniel's faith in God was so great that it finally brought about his freedom and his appointment to a high office in the government of his country [Daniel 6:13-28].

This story was written for you to instruct you in the art of freeing yourself from any problem or prison in the world.

Most of us on finding ourselves in the lions' den would be concerned only with the lions; we would not be thinking of any other problem in the whole wide world but that of lions. Yet, we are told that Daniel turned his back upon them and looked toward the light that was God. If we could follow the example of Daniel while threatened with any dire disaster such as lions, poverty or sickness, if, like Daniel, we could remove our attention to the light that is God, our solutions would be similarly simple.

For example, if you were imprisoned, no man would need to tell you that what you should desire is freedom. Freedom or rather the desire to be free would be automatic. The same would be true if you found yourself sick or in debt or in any other predicament.

Lions represent seemingly unsoluble situations of a threatening nature.

Every problem automatically produces its solution in the form of a desire to be free from the problem.

Therefore, turn your back upon your problem and focus your attention upon the desired solution by already feeling yourself to be that which you desire.

Continue in this belief, and you will find that your prison wall will disappear as you begin to express that which you have become conscious of being.

I have seen people, apparently hopelessly in debt, apply this principle, and in but a very short time, debts that were mountainous were removed. I have also seen those whom doctors had given up as uncurable apply this principle, and in an incredibly short time, their so-called incurable disease vanished and left no scar.

Look upon your desires as the spoken words of God and every word of prophecy of that which you are capable of being. Do not question whether you are worthy or unworthy to realize these desires. Accept them as they come to you. Give thanks for them as though they were gifts. Feel happy and grateful for having received such wonderful gifts. Then go your way in peace.

Such simple acceptance of your desires is like the dropping of fertile seed into an ever-prepared soil.

When you drop your desire in consciousness as a seed, confident that it shall appear in its full-blown potential, you have done all that is expected of you. To be worried or concerned about the manner of their unfoldment is to hold these fertile seeds in a mental grasp and, therefore, to prevent them from really maturing to full harvest.

Don't be anxious or concerned as to results. Results will follow just as surely as day follows night.

Have faith in this planting until the evidence is manifest to you that it is so. Your confidence in this procedure will pay great rewards. You wait but a little while in the consciousness of the thing desired;

then suddenly, and when you least expect it, the thing felt becomes your expression. Life is no respecter of persons [Acts 10:34; Romans 2:11] and destroys nothing; it continues to keep alive that which man is conscious of being.

Things will disappear only as man changes his consciousness. Deny it if you will, it still remains a fact that consciousness is the only reality and things but mirror that which you are conscious of being.

The heavenly state you seek will be found only in consciousness for the Kingdom of Heaven is within you.

Your consciousness is the only living reality, the eternal head of creation. That which you are conscious of being is the temporal body that you wear.

To turn your attention from that which you are aware of being is to decapitate that body; but, just as a chicken or snake continues to jump and throb for a while after its head has been removed, likewise qualities and conditions appear to live for a while after your attention has been taken from them.

Man, not knowing this law of consciousness, constantly gives thought to his previous habitual conditions and, through being attentive to them, places upon these dead bodies the eternal head of creation; thereby he reanimates and re-resurrects them.

You must leave these dead bodies alone and let the dead bury the dead [Matthew 8:22, Luke 9:60].

Man, having put his hand to the plough (that is, after assuming the consciousness of the quality desired), by looking back, can only defeat his fitness for the Kingdom of Heaven [Luke 9:62].

As the will of heaven is ever done on earth, you are today in the heaven that you have established within yourself, for here on this very earth your heaven reveals itself.

The Kingdom of Heaven really is at hand. Now is the accepted time. So create a new heaven, enter into a new state of consciousness and a new earth will appear.

CHAPTER 22

Fishing

They went forth, and entered into a ship, and that night they caught nothing.

—John 21:3

And He said unto them, Cast the net on the right side of the ship, and ye shall find. They cast therefore, and now they were not able to draw it for the multitude of fishes.

—John 21:6

It is recorded that the disciples fished all night and caught nothing. Then Jesus appeared upon the scene and told them to cast their nets again, but, this time, to cast them on the right side. Peter obeyed the voice of Jesus and cast his nets once more into the waters. Where but a moment before the water was completely empty of fish, the nets almost broke with the number of the resulting catch [John 21:3-6].

Man, fishing all through the night of human ignorance, attempts to realize his desires through effort and struggle only to find in the end that his search is fruitless. When man discovers his awareness of being to be Christ Jesus, he will obey its voice and let it direct his fishing. He will cast his hook on the right side; he will apply the law in the right manner and will seek in consciousness for the thing desired. Finding it there, he will know that it will be multiplied in the world of form.

Those who have had the pleasure of fishing know what a thrill it is to feel the fish upon the hook. The bite of the fish is followed by the play of the fish; this play, in turn, is followed by the landing of the fish.

Something similar takes place in the consciousness of man as he fishes for the manifestations of life.

Fishermen know that if they wish to catch big fish, they must fish in deep waters; if you would catch a large measure of life, you must leave behind you the shallow waters with its many reefs and barriers and launch out into the deep blue waters where the big ones play.

To catch the large manifestations of life you must enter into deeper and freer states of consciousness; only in these depths do the big expressions of life live.

Here is a simple formula for successful fishing.

First, decide what it is you want to express or possess. This is essential.

You must definitely know what you want of life before you can fish for it. After your decision is made, turn from the world of sense, remove your attention from the problem and place it on just being, by repeating quietly but with feeling, "I AM".

As your attention is removed from the world round about you and placed upon the I AM, so that you are lost in the feeling of simply being, you will find yourself slipping the anchor that tied you to the shallows of your problem; and effortlessly you will find yourself moving out into the deep.

The sensation which accompanies this act is one of expansion. You will feel yourself rise and expand as though you were actually growing. Do not be afraid of this floating, growing experience for you are not going to die to anything but your limitations.

However, your limitations are going to die as you move away from them for they live only in your consciousness.

In this deep or expanded consciousness, you will feel yourself to be a mighty pulsating power as deep and as rhythmical as the ocean. This expanded feeling is the signal that you are now in the deep blue waters where the big fish swim. Suppose the fish you decided to catch were health and freedom; you begin to fish in this formless pulsating depth of yourself for these qualities or states of consciousness by feeling "I AM healthy" , "I AM free".

You continue claiming and feeling yourself to be healthy and free until the conviction that you are so possesses you. As the conviction is born within you, so that all doubts pass away and you know and feel that you are free from the limitations of the past, you will know that you have hooked these fish.

The joy which courses through your entire being on feeling that you are that which you desired to be is equal to the thrill of the fisherman as he hooks his fish.

Now comes the play of the fish. This is accomplished by returning to the world of the senses.

As you open your eyes on the world round about you, the conviction and the consciousness that you are healthy and free should be so established within you that your whole being thrills in anticipation.

Then, as you walk through the necessary interval of time that it will take the things felt to embody themselves, you will feel a secret thrill in knowing that in a little while that which no man sees, but that which you feel and know that you are, will be landed.

In a moment when you think not, while you faithfully walk in this consciousness, you will begin to express and possess that which you are conscious of being and possessing; experiencing with the fisherman the joy of landing the big one.

Now, go and fish for the manifestations of life by casting your nets in the right side.

CHAPTER 23

Be Ears That Hear

Let these sayings sink down into your ears; For the Son of Man shall be delivered into the hands of men.

—Luke 9:44

Be not as those who have eyes that see not and ears that hear not. Let these revelations sink deep into your ears, for after the Son (idea) is conceived, man with his false values (reason) will attempt to explain the why and wherefore of the Son's expression, and in so doing, will rend him to pieces.

After men have agreed that a certain thing is humanly impossible and therefore cannot be done, let someone accomplish the impossible thing; the wise ones who said it could not be done will begin to tell you why and how it happened. After they are all through tearing the seamless robe [John 19:23] (cause of manifestation) apart, they will be as far from the truth as they were when they proclaimed it impossible. As long as man looks for the cause of expression in places other than the expresser, he looks in vain.

For thousands of years, man has been told:

I AM the resurrection and the life.

—John 11:25

No manifestation cometh unto me save I draw it.

—John 6:44

But man will not believe it. He prefers to believe in causes outside of himself.

The moment that which was not seen becomes seen, man is ready to explain the cause and purpose of its appearance.

Thus, the Son of Man (idea desiring manifestation) is constantly being destroyed at the hands of man (reasonable explanation or wisdom).

Now that your awareness is revealed to you as cause of all expression, do not return to the darkness of Egypt with its many gods. There is but one God. The one and only God is your awareness.

> *And all the inhabitants of the earth are reputed as nothing. And He doeth according to His will in the army of Heaven and among the inhabitants of the earth, and none can stay His hand, or say unto him 'what doest Thou?'*
>
> *All the inhabitants of the earth are accounted as nothing; but He does according to His will in the host of heaven and among the inhabitants of earth. And no one can ward off His hand or say to Him, 'What have You done?'*
>
> —Daniel 4:35

If the whole world should agree that a certain thing could not be expressed and yet you became aware of being that which they had agreed could not be expressed, you would express it.

Your awareness never asks permission to express that which you are aware of being. It does so, naturally and without effort, in spite of the wisdom of man and all opposition.

> *Salute no man by the way.*
>
> *Carry no money belt, no bag, no shoes; and greet no one on the way.*
>
> —Luke 10:4; 2Kings 4:29

This is not a command to be insolent or unfriendly, but a reminder not to recognize a superior, not to see in anyone a barrier to your expression.

None can stay your hand or question your ability to express that which you are conscious of being.

Do not judge after the appearances of a thing, "for all are as nothing in the eyes of God."

> *All the nations are as nothing before Him. They are regarded by Him as less than nothing and meaningless.*
>
> —Isaiah 40:17

When the disciples, through their judgment of appearances, saw the insane child [Mark 9:17-29; Luke 9:37-43], they thought it a more difficult problem to solve than others they had seen; and so they failed to achieve a cure.

In judging after appearances, they forgot that all things were possible to God [Matthew 19:26; Mark 10:27]. Hypnotized as they were by the reality of appearances, they could not feel the naturalness of sanity.

The only way for you to avoid such failures is to constantly bear in mind that your awareness is the Almighty, the all-wise presence. Without help, this unknown presence within you effortlessly outpictures that which you are aware of being.

Be perfectly indifferent to the evidence of the senses, so that you may feel the naturalness of your desire, and your desire will be realized. Turn from appearances and feel the naturalness of that perfect perception within yourself, a quality never to be distrusted or doubted. Its understanding will never lead you astray.

Your desire is the solution of your problem. As the desire is realized, the problem is dissolved.

You cannot force anything outwardly by the mightiest effort of the will. There is only one way you can command the things you want and that is by assuming the consciousness of the things desired.

There is a vast difference between feeling a thing and merely knowing it intellectually. You must accept without reservation the fact that by possessing (feeling) a thing in consciousness, you have commanded the reality that causes it to come into existence in concrete form.

You must be absolutely convinced of an unbroken connection between the invisible reality and its visible manifestation. Your inner acceptance must become an intense, unalterable conviction which transcends both reason and intellect, renouncing entirely any belief in the reality of the externalization except as a reflection of an inner state of consciousness. When you really understand and believe these things, you will have built up so profound a certainty that nothing can shake you.

Your desires are the invisible realities which respond only to the commands of God. God commands the invisible to appear by claiming himself to be the thing commanded.

> *He made Himself equal with God and found it not robbery to do the works of God.*
>
> —Philippians 2:6

Now let this saying sink deep in your ear:

BE CONSCIOUS OF BEING THAT WHICH YOU WANT TO APPEAR.

CHAPTER 24

Clairvoyance

Having eyes, see ye not? And having ears, hear ye not? And do ye not remember?

—Mark 8:18

True clairvoyance rests, not in your ability to see things beyond the range of human vision, but rather in your ability to understand that which you see.

A financial statement can be seen by anyone, but very few can read a financial statement. The capacity to interpret the statement is the mark of clear seeing or clairvoyance.

That every object, both animate and inanimate, is enveloped in a liquid light which moves and pulsates with an energy far more radiant than the objects themselves, no one knows better than the author; but he also knows that the ability to see such auras is not equal to the ability to understand that which one sees in the world around about him.

To illustrate this point, here is a story with which the whole world is familiar, yet only the true mystic or clairvoyant has ever really seen it.

SYNOPSIS

The story of Dumas' "Count of Monte Cristo" is, to the mystic and true clairvoyant, the biography of every man.

I

Edmond Dantés, a young sailor, finds the captain of his ship dead. Taking command of the ship in the midst of a storm-swept sea, he attempts to steer the ship into a safe anchorage.

COMMENTARY

Life itself is a storm-swept sea with which man wrestles as he tries to steer himself into a haven of rest.

II

On Dantés is a secret document which must be given to a man he does not know, but who will make himself known to the young sailor in due time. This document is a plan to set the Emperor Napoleon free from his prison on the Isle of Elba.

COMMENTARY

Within every man is the secret plan that will set free the mighty emperor within himself.

III

As Dantés reaches port, three men (who by their flattery and praise have succeeded in worming their way into the good graces of the present king), fearing any change that would alter their positions in the government, have the young mariner arrested and committed to the catacombs.

COMMENTARY

Man in his attempt to find security in this world is misled by the false lights of greed, vanity and power.

Most men believe that fame, great wealth or political power would secure them against the storms of life. So they seek to acquire these as the anchors of their life, only to find that in their search for these they gradually lose the knowledge of their true being. If man places his faith in things other than himself, that in which his faith is placed, will in time destroy him; at which time he will be as one imprisoned in confusion and despair.

IV

Here in this tomb, Dantés is forgotten and left to rot. Many years pass. Then one day, Dantés (who is by this time a living skeleton) hears a knock on his wall. Answering this knock, he hears the voice of one on the other side of the stone. In response to this voice, Dantés removes the stone and discovers an old priest who has been in prison so long that no one knows the reason for his imprisonment or the length of time he has been there.

COMMENTARY

Here behind these walls of mental darkness, man remains in what appears to be a living death. After years of disappointment, man turns from these false friends, and he discovers within himself the ancient one (his awareness of being) who has been buried since the day he first believed himself to be man and forgot that he was God.

V

The old priest had spent many years digging his way out of this living tomb only to discover that he had dug his way into Dantés' tomb. He then resigns himself to his fate and decides to find his joy and freedom by instructing Dantés in all that he knows concerning the mysteries of life and to aid him to escape as well.

Dantés, at first, is impatient to acquire all this information; but the old priest, with infinite patience garnered through his long imprisonment, shows Dantés how unfit he is to receive this knowledge in his present, unprepared, anxious mind. So, with philosophic calm, he slowly reveals to the young man the mysteries of life and time.

COMMENTARY

This revelation is so wonderful that when man first hears it he wants to acquire it all at once; but he finds that, after numberless years spent in the belief of being man, he has so completely forgotten his true identity that he is now incapable of absorbing this memory all at once. He also discovers that he can do so only in proportion to his letting go of all human values and opinions.

VI

As Dantés ripens under the old priest's instructions, the old man finds himself living more and more in the consciousness of Dantés. Finally, he imparts his last bit of wisdom to Dantés, making him competent to handle positions of trust. He then tells him of an inexhaustible treasure buried on the Isle of Monte Cristo.

COMMENTARY

As man drops these cherished human values, he absorbs more and more of the light (the old priest), until finally he becomes the light and knows himself to be the ancient one. I AM the light of the world.

VII

At this revelation, the walls of the catacomb which separated them from the ocean above cave in, crushing the old man to death. The guards, discovering the accident, sew the old priest's body into a sack and prepare to cast it out to sea. As they leave to get a stretcher, Dantés removes the body of the old priest and sews himself into the bag. The guards, unaware of this change of bodies, and believing him to be the old man, throw Dantés into the water.

COMMENTARY

The flowing of both blood and water in the death of the old priest is comparable to the flow of blood and water from the side of Jesus as the Roman soldiers pierced him, the phenomenon which always takes place at birth (here symbolizing the birth of a higher consciousness).

VIII

Dantés frees himself from the sack, goes to the Isle of Monte Cristo and discovers the buried treasure. Then, armed with this fabulous wealth and this superhuman wisdom, he discards his human identity of Edmond Dantés and assumes the title of the Count of Monte Cristo.

COMMENTARY

Man discovers his awareness of being to be the inexhaustible treasure of the universe. In that day, when man makes this discovery, he dies as man and awakes as God.

Yes, Edmond Dantés becomes the Count of Monte Cristo. Man becomes Christ.

CHAPTER 25

Twenty Third Psalm

I

The Lord is my Shepherd; I shall not want.

COMMENTARY

My awareness is my Lord and Shepherd. That which I AM aware of being is the sheep that follow me. So good a shepherd is my awareness of being, it has never lost one sheep or thing that I AM aware of being.

My consciousness is a voice calling in the wilderness of human confusion; calling all that I AM conscious of being to follow me.

So well do my sheep know my voice, they have never failed to respond to my call; nor will there come a time when that which I am convinced that I AM will fail to find me.

I AM an open door for all that I AM to enter.

My awareness of being is Lord and Shepherd of my life. Now I know I shall never be in need of proof or lack the evidence of that which I am aware of being. Knowing this, I shall become aware of being great, loving, wealthy, healthy and all other attributes that I admire.

II

He maketh me to lie down in green pastures.

COMMENTARY

My awareness of being magnifies all that I am aware of being, so there is ever an abundance of that which I am conscious of being.

It makes no difference what it is that man is conscious of being, he will find it eternally springing in his world.

The Lord's measure (man's conception of himself) is always pressed down, shaken together and running over.

III

He leadeth me beside the still waters.

COMMENTARY

There is no need to fight for that which I am conscious of being, for all that I am conscious of being shall be led to me as effortlessly as a shepherd leads his flock to the still waters of a quiet spring.

IV

He restoreth my soul; He leadeth me in the paths of righteousness for His Name's sake.

COMMENTARY

Now that my memory is restored – so that I know I AM the Lord and beside me there is no God – my kingdom is restored.

My kingdom – which became dismembered in the day that I believed in powers apart from myself – is now fully restored.

Now that I know my awareness of being is God, I shall make the right use of this knowledge by becoming aware of being that which I desire to be.

V

Yea, though I walk through the valley of the shadow of death, I will fear no evil; for Thou art with me; Thy rod and Thy staff, they comfort me.

COMMENTARY

Yes, though I walk through all the confusion and changing opinions of men, I will fear no evil, for I have found consciousness to be that which makes the confusion. Having in my own case restored it to its rightful place and dignity, I shall, in spite of the confusion, outpicture that which I am now conscious of being. And the very confusion will echo and reflect my own dignity.

VI

Thou preparest a table before me in the presence of mine enemies; Thou anointest my head with oil; my cup runneth over.

COMMENTARY

In the face of seeming opposition and conflict, I shall succeed, for I will continue to outpicture the abundance that I am now conscious of being.

My head (consciousness) will continue to overflow with the joy of being God.

VII

Surely goodness and mercy shall follow me all the days of my life; and I will dwell in the house of the Lord forever.

COMMENTARY

Because I am now conscious of being good and merciful, signs of goodness and mercy are compelled to follow me all the days of my life, for I will continue to dwell in the house (or consciousness) of being God (good) forever.

CHAPTER 26

Gethsemane

Then cometh Jesus with them unto a place called Gethsemane, and saith unto the disciples, Sit ye here, while I go and pray yonder.

—Matt. 26:36

A most wonderful mystical romance is told in the story of Jesus in the Garden of Gethsemane, but man has failed to see the light of its symbology and has mistakenly interpreted this mystical union as an agonizing experience in which Jesus pleaded in vain with His Father to change His destiny.

Gethsemane is, to the mystic, the Garden of Creation – the place in consciousness where man goes to realize his defined objectives. Gethsemane is a compound word meaning to press out an oily substance; Geth, to press out, and Shemen, an oily substance.

The story of Gethsemane reveals to the mystic, in dramatic symbology, the act of creation.

Just as man contains within himself an oily substance which, in the act of creation, is pressed out into a likeness of himself, so he has within himself a divine principle (his consciousness) which conditions itself as a state of consciousness and without assistance presses out or objectifies itself.

A garden is a cultivated piece of ground, a specially prepared field, where seeds of the gardener's own choice are planted and cultivated.

Gethsemane is such a garden, the place in consciousness where the mystic goes with his properly defined objectives. This garden is entered when man takes his attention from the world round about him and places it on his objectives.

Man's clarified desires are seeds containing the power and plans of self-expression and, like the seeds within man, these, too, are buried within an oily substance (a joyful, thankful attitude of mind).

As man contemplates being and possessing that which he desires to be and to possess, he has begun the process of pressing out or the spiritual act of creation.

These seeds are pressed out and planted when man loses himself in a wild, mad state of joy, consciously feeling and claiming himself to be that which he formerly desired to be.

Desires expressed, or pressed out, result in the passing of that particular desire. Man cannot possess a thing and still desire to possess it at one and the same time. So, as one consciously appropriates the feeling of being the thing desired, this desire to be the thing passes – is realized.

The receptive attitude of mind, feeling, and receiving the impression of being the thing desired, is the fertile ground or womb which receives the seed (defined objective).

The seed which is pressed out of a man grows into the likeness of the man from whom it was pressed.

Likewise, the mystical seed, your conscious claim that you are that which you heretofore desired to be, will grow into the likeness of you from whom and into whom it is pressed.

Yes, Gethsemane is the cultivated garden of romance where the disciplined man goes to press seeds of joy (defined desires) out of himself into his receptive attitude of mind, there to care for and nurture them by consciously walking in the joy of being all that formerly he desired to be.

Feel with the Great Gardener the secret thrill of knowing that things and qualities not now seen will be seen as soon as these conscious impressions grow and ripen to maturity.

Your consciousness is Lord and Husband [Isaiah 54:5]; the conscious state in which you dwell is wife or beloved. This state made visible is your son bearing witness of you, his father and mother, for your visible world is made in the image and likeness [Genesis 2:26] of the state of consciousness in which you live; your world and the fullness thereof are nothing more or less than your defined consciousness objectified.

Knowing this to be true, see to it that you choose well the mother of your children – that conscious state in which you live, your conception of yourself.

The wise man chooses his wife with great discretion. He realizes that his children must inherit the qualities of their parents and so he devotes much time and care to the selection of their mother. The mystic knows that the conscious state in which he lives is the choice that he has made of a wife, the mother of his children, that this state must in time embody itself within his world; so he is ever select in his choice and always claims himself to be his highest ideal.

He consciously defines himself as that which he desires to be.

When man realizes that the conscious state in which he lives is the choice that he has made of a mate, he will be more careful of his moods and feelings. He will not permit himself to react to suggestions of fear, lack or any undesirable impression. Such suggestions of lack could never pass the watch of the disciplined mind of the mystic, for he knows that every conscious claim must in time be expressed as a condition of his world – of his environment.

So, he remains faithful to his beloved, his defined objective, by defining and claiming and feeling himself to be that which he desires to express. Let a man ask himself if his defined objective would be a thing of joy and beauty if it were realized.

If his answer is in the affirmative, then he may know that his choice of a bride is a princess of Israel, a daughter of Judah, for every defined objective which expresses joy when realized is a daughter of Judah, the king of praise.

Jesus took with Him into His hour of prayer His disciples, or disciplined attributes of mind, and commanded them to watch while He prayed, so that no thought or belief that would deny the realization of His desire might enter His consciousness.

Follow the example of Jesus, who, with His desires clearly defined, entered the Garden of Gethsemane (the state of joy) accompanied by His disciples (His disciplined mind) to lose Himself in a wild joy of realization.

The fixing of His attention on His objective was His command to His disciplined mind to watch and remain faithful to that fixation. Contemplating the joy that would be His on realizing His desire, He began the spiritual act of generation, the act of pressing out the mystical seed – His defined desire. In this fixation He remained, claiming and feeling Himself to be that which He (before He entered Gethsemane) desired to be, until His whole being (consciousness) was bathed in an oily sweat (joy) resembling blood (life); in short, until His whole consciousness was permeated with the living, sustained joy of being His defined objective.

As this fixation is accomplished so that the mystic knows by his feeling of joy that he has passed from his former conscious state into his present consciousness, the Passover or Crucifixion is attained.

This crucifixion or fixation of the new conscious claim is followed by the Sabbath, a time of rest. There is always an interval of time between the impression and its expression, between the conscious claim and its embodiment. This interval is called the Sabbath, the period of rest or non-effort (the day of entombment).

To walk unmoved in the consciousness of being or possessing a certain state is to keep the Sabbath.

The story of the crucifixion beautifully expresses this mystical stillness or rest. We are told that after Jesus cried out, "It is finished!" [John 19:30], He was placed in a tomb. There He remained for the entire Sabbath.

When the new state or consciousness is appropriated so, you feel by this appropriation fixed and secure in the knowledge that it is finished; then you, too, will cry out, "It is finished!" and will enter the tomb or Sabbath, an interval of time in which you will walk unmoved in the conviction that your new consciousness must be resurrected (made visible).

Easter, the day of resurrection, falls on the first Sunday after the full moon in Aries. The mystical reason for this is simple. A defined area will not precipitate itself in the form of rain until this area reaches the point of saturation; just so the state in which you dwell will not express itself until the whole is permeated with the consciousness that it is so – it is finished.

Your defined objective is the imaginary state, just as the equator is the imaginary line across which the sun must pass to mark the beginning of spring. This state, like the moon, has no light or life of itself; but will reflect the light of consciousness or sun.

I am the light of the world.

—Matthew 5:14; John 8:12; John 9:5; John 12:46

I am the resurrection and the life.

—John 11:25

As Easter is determined by the full moon in Aries, so too is the resurrection of your conscious claim determined by the full consciousness of your claim, by actually living as this new conception.

Most men fail to resurrect their objectives because they fail to remain faithful to their newly defined state until this fullness is attained.

If man would bear in mind the fact that there can be no Easter or day of resurrection until after the full moon, he would realize that the state into which he has consciously passed will be expressed or resurrected only after he has remained within the state of being his defined objective.

Until his whole self thrills with the feeling of actually being his conscious claim — in consciously living in this state of being it and only in this way – will man ever resurrect or realize his desire.

CHAPTER 27

A Formula for Victory

Every place that the sole of your foot shall tread upon, that have I given unto you.

—Joshua 1:3

The majority of people are familiar with the story of Joshua capturing the city of Jericho. What they do not know is that this story is the perfect formula for Victory, under any circumstances and against all odds.

It is recorded that Joshua was armed only with the knowledge that every place that the sole of his foot should tread upon would be given to him; that he desired to capture or tread upon the city of Jericho but found the walls separating him from the city impassable.

It seemed physically impossible for Joshua to get beyond these massive walls and stand upon the city of Jericho. Yet, he was driven by the knowledge of the promise that, regardless of the barriers and obstacles separating him from his desires, if he could but stand upon the city, it would be given to him.

The Book of Joshua further records that instead of fighting this giant problem of the wall, Joshua employed the services of the harlot, Rahab, and sent her as a spy into the city. As Rahab entered her house, which stood in the midst of the city, Joshua – who was securely barred by the impassable walls of Jericho – blew on his trumpet seven times. At the seventh blast, the walls crumbled and Joshua entered the city victoriously.

To the uninitiated, this story is senseless. To the one who sees it as a psychological drama, rather than as a historical record, it is most revealing.

If we would follow the example of Joshua, our victory would be similarly simple.

Joshua symbolizes to you, the reader, your present state; the city of Jericho symbolizes your desire, or defined objective.

The walls of Jericho symbolize the obstacles between you and the realization of your objectives. The foot symbolizes the understanding; placing the sole of the foot upon a definite place indicates fixing a definite psychological state.

Rahab, the spy, is your ability to travel secretly or psychologically to any place in space. Consciousness knows no frontier. No one can stop you from dwelling psychologically at any point, or in any state in time or space.

Regardless of the physical barriers separating you from your objective, you can, without effort or help of anyone, annihilate time, space and barriers.

Thus, you can dwell, psychologically, in the desired state. So, although you may not be able to tread physically upon a state or city, you can always tread psychologically upon any desired state. By treading psychologically, I mean that you can now, this moment, close your eyes, and after visualizing or imagining a place or state other than your present one, actually FEEL that you are now in such a place or state. You can feel this condition to be so real that upon opening your eyes you are amazed to find that you are not physically there.

A harlot, as you know, gives to all men that which they ask of her. Rahab, the harlot, symbolizes your infinite capacity to psychologically assume any desirable state without questioning whether or not you are physically or morally fit to do so.

You can today capture the modern city of Jericho or your defined objective if you will psychologically re-enact this story of Joshua; but to capture the city and realize your desires, you must carefully follow the formula of victory as laid down in this book of Joshua.

This is the application of this victorious formula as a modem mystic reveals it today:

> First: Define your objective—not the manner of obtaining it, but your objective, pure and simple; know exactly what it is you desire so that you have a clear mental picture of it.
>
> Secondly: Take your attention away from the obstacles which separate you from your objective and place your thought on the objective itself.
>
> Thirdly: Close your eyes and FEEL that you are already in the city or state that you would capture. Remain within this psychological state until you get a conscious reaction of complete satisfaction in this victory. Then, by simply opening your eyes, return to your former conscious state.

This secret journey into the desired state, with its subsequent psychological reaction of complete satisfaction, is all that is necessary to bring about total victory.

This victorious psychical state will embody itself despite all opposition. It has the plan and power of self-expression.

From this point forward, follow the example of Joshua, who, after psychologically dwelling in the desired state until he received a complete conscious reaction of victory, did nothing more to bring about this victory than to blow seven times on his trumpet.

The seventh blast symbolizes the seventh day, a time of stillness or rest, the interval between the subjective and objective states, a period of pregnancy or joyful expectancy.

This stillness is not the stillness of the body but rather the stillness of the mind – a perfect passivity, which is not indolence but a living stillness born of trust in this immutable law of consciousness.

Those not familiar with this law or formula for victory, in attempting to still their minds, succeed only in acquiring a quiet tension, which is nothing more than compressed anxiety.

But you, who know this law, will find that after capturing the psychological state which would be yours if you were already victoriously and actually entrenched in that city, will move forward towards the physical realization of your desires.

You will do this without doubt or fear, in a state of mind fixed in the knowledge of a pre-arranged victory.

You will not be afraid of the enemy, because the outcome has been determined by the psychological state that preceded the physical offensive; and all the forces of heaven and earth cannot stop the victorious fulfillment of that state.

Stand still in the psychological state defined as your objective until you feel the thrill of Victory.

Then, with confidence born of the knowledge of this law, watch the physical realization of your objective.

> *Set your self, stand still, and watch the salvation of the Lord with you...*
>
> —2 Chronicles 20:17